Please renew or return items by the date shown on your receipt

www.hertsdirect.org/libraries

Renewals and enquiries: 0300 123 4049

Textphone for hearing or speech impaired 0300 123 4041

D1471784

METHUEN DRAMA

H46 621 401 0

Methuen Drama Student Edition

10 9 8 7 6 5 4 3 2 1

This edition first published in the United Kingdom in 2009 by
Methuen Drama
A & C Black Publishers Ltd
36 Soho Square
London W1D 3QY
www.methuendrama.com

Fear and Misery of the Third Reich originally published in this translation by
Methuen in 1983 by arrangement with Suhrkamp Verlag, Frankfurt am Main
Translation copyright © 1983 by Stefan S. Brecht
Original work entitled *Furcht und Elend des Dritten Reiches* copyright © 1957 by
Suhrkamp Verlag, Berlin

Commentary and notes copyright © 2009 by Tom Kuhn and Charlotte Ryland

A CIP catalogue record for this book is available from the British Library

ISBN 978 1 408 10008 0

Thanks are due as follows for permission to reproduce the illustrations: for
1, Akademie der Künste, Bertolt Brecht Archiv (every effort has been made to
identify a copyright holder). 2, Akademie der Künste, Bertolt Brecht Archiv:
Fotoarchiv (photographer unknown), by kind permission of the Brecht heirs. 3, by
kind permission of the Erbengemeinschaft Professor Caspar Neher. 4, Akademie
der Künste, Bertolt Brecht Archiv: Theaterdokumentation; photograph by Gerda
Goedhart, by kind permission of the Brecht heirs.

Typeset by Deltatype Ltd, Birkenhead, Wirral
Printed and bound in Great Britain by CPI Cox & Wyman, Reading, Berkshire

Contents

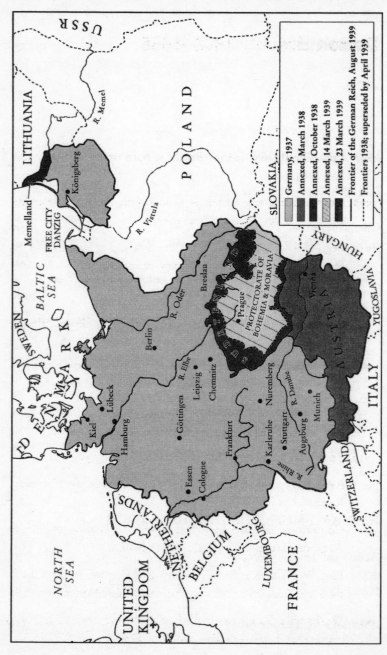

The Third Reich in the 1930s

Bertolt Brecht: 1898–1956

1898 Eugen Berthold Friedrich Brecht is born on 10 February in Augsburg.

1908 Goes to Augsburg Grammar School. Caspar Neher (later his designer) is one of his closest friends.

1914 Begins to write poems, stories, reviews and essays for the literary supplement of a local newspaper.

First World War breaks out.

1915 Caspar Neher volunteers for military service. Brecht writes to him regularly.

1916 Almost expelled for unpatriotic essay on the title: 'It is a sweet and honourable thing to die for one's country'.

The Battle of Verdun. Generals von Hindenburg and von Ludendorff take overall command.

1917 Enrols as medical student at Munich University.

Revolution in Russia. Russia makes peace with the German Reich.

1918 Conscripted into the army and serves as a medical orderly at Augsburg Military Hospital. Writes *Baal*.

First World War ends. Declaration of a German Republic by the Social Democrats. Foundation of the German Communist Party.

1919 Works with Neher to establish as many literary and artistic contacts as possible. First version of *Drums in the Night*.

Adolf Hitler joins the German Workers' Party (DAP).
The Versailles Treaty seals peace after the First World War.
Economic and military sanctions on Germany, including
restrictions on military forces, loss of territories such as the
Rhineland, and payment of reparations. Weimar Republic
established, a parliamentary democracy with an elected
President and a Chancellor.

1920 Visits Berlin.

Founding of the National Socialist German Workers' Party
(NSDAP). Kapp Putsch attempts to overthrow Weimar
Republic.

1921 Brecht and Neher in financial difficulties. Brecht ends up in
hospital suffering from malnutrition.

The *Sturmabteilung* (SA), the paramilitary wing of the
NSDAP, is founded (also referred to as the 'Brownshirts').

1922 Wins the Kleist Prize for *Drums in the Night*.

German army crushes Soviet Republic of Saxony.

1923 Activities of Hitler's National Socialists are hotly discussed
in Brecht's Munich circle. First productions of *In the Jungle
of the Cities* and *Baal*. Meets Helene Weigel, the actress, for
the first time.

On 8–9 November in Munich, Hitler's attempt to overthrow
the government (the so-called Beerhall Putsch) fails.

1924 Settles in Berlin and is taken on as dramaturg (literary
adviser) at Max Reinhardt's Deutsches Theater. Meets
Elisabeth Hauptmann who becomes his constant collaborator.

Hitler sentenced to five years' imprisonment at Landsberg on
1 April. He serves only eight months. In prison completes a draft
of the first volume of his treatise *Mein Kampf* (*My Struggle*).

1925 Joins 'Group 25', aiming to co-ordinate the interests of younger authors not represented by literary groups dominated by the older generation.

NSDAP re-established. Hindenburg elected President of the Weimar Republic. The *Schutzstaffel* (SS) founded as Hitler's élite personal guard.

1926 *Man equals Man* premiered. Begins to study the theories of Karl Marx, as the only adequate method of analysing the workings of capitalism.

In July the Nazi youth movement is named the 'Hitler Jugend' (Hitler Youth), and becomes part of the SA.

1927 Publication of *Hauspostille* (poems). Works with Erwin Piscator, the pioneer of Communist political theatre in Germany, on a dramatisation of Hašek's novel, *The Good Soldier Schweik*. First collaboration with Kurt Weill, on *Mahagonny*, with designs by Neher.

1928 *The Threepenny Opera* opens at Theater am Schiffbauerdamm and is the hit of the season.

The Nazis receive only 2.6% of the vote in the Reichstag (parliamentary) elections.

1929 Marries Helene Weigel. Writes first 'learning plays'.

The stockmarket in the United States collapses on 29 October, triggering a widespread economic depression that has serious consequences for Germany.

1930 The first performance of *The Rise and Fall of the City of Mahagonny*, an opera with words by Brecht and music by Kurt Weill, causes a riot as the Nazis voice their criticism at Leipzig. In his notes on the opera, Brecht lists the differences between the traditional *dramatic* (or Aristotelian) and the new *epic* (or non-Aristotelian) theatre at which he is aiming. First performance of the learning play, *The Measures Taken*.

The Nazis poll 18.3% in the September Reichstag elections. The League of German Girls (BDM), the female branch of the Nazi youth movement, is founded.

1931   Film version of *The Threepenny Opera*, directed by Georg Wilhelm Pabst.

In December, unemployment in Germany reaches 5.6 million.

1932   Brecht's only film *Kuhle Wampe* is held up by the censor. His dramatisation of Maxim Gorky's novel *The Mother* is performed by a left-wing collective in Berlin, with music by Hanns Eisler, and demonstrates the development of a worker's mother towards proletarian class-consciousness. Studies Marxism under dissident Communist Karl Korsch.

Hitler is defeated by President Hindenburg in two presidential elections in March and April. In the July Reichstag elections, the Nazis poll 37.4%, making them the largest party in Germany. In August, Hindenburg rejects Hitler's bid to become Chancellor, and in Reichstag elections on 6 November the Nazi vote declines to 33.1%. In December, General Schleicher becomes Chancellor.

1933   The night after the Reichstag Fire, Brecht flees with his family to Prague. He moves to Vienna, then Zurich, finally settling on the island of Fyn in Denmark. Premiere of *The Seven Deadly Sins* in Paris.

Schleicher resigns as Chancellor on 28 January, and on 30 January Hindenburg appoints Hitler Chancellor in a coalition government. On 27 February the Reichstag building in Berlin burns down. The Communists are blamed. The following day a

'Reichstag Fire decree' is passed by presidential decree, suspending civil liberties and allowing for an extended state of emergency. The last Reichstag election in a multi-party state held on 5 March. The NSDAP gains a slim majority with the DNVP (43.9%). The Enabling Law is passed on 24 March, which allows the government to legislate without parliamentary involvement, and so provides the basis for Hitler's dictatorship. On 1 April a boycott of Jewish businesses and professionals is pronounced. Labour leaders arrested and unions destroyed, replaced by the new German Labour Front (DAF). Dissolution of all political parties (except NSDAP). On 12 November, the first Reichstag elections in the new one-party state are held. The NSDAP gains 95.2% of the votes.

1934　Writes *The Threepenny Novel*, a more obviously Marxist version of *The Threepenny Opera*. Redrafts, with Hanns Eisler and Margarete Steffin, *Round Heads and Pointed Heads or Empires of a Feather Flock Together. An atrocity fairy tale.* Walter Benjamin stays with Brecht. Visits London. Themes of flight and exile enter his poems.

The Law for the Reconstruction of the Reich suspends the powers of regional governments. Hitler conducts a purge against his political opponents. SA leader Ernst Röhm is murdered. The SS increases in power and becomes an independent organisation. When President Hindenburg dies in August, Hitler merges offices of Chancellor and President, becoming head of state as well as commander-in-chief.

1935　Visits Moscow, talks to Soviet dramatist Sergei Tretiakov about the 'alienation effect'. Attends International Writers' Conference in Paris. Brecht is stripped of his German citizenship by the Nazis. Visits New York to look in on a production of *The Mother* which does not meet with his approval.

In March, military conscription is reintroduced. In June
compulsory labour service is established for men aged eighteen
to twenty-five. On 15 September, the Nuremberg Race Laws are
promulgated, prohibiting marriage between Jews and non-Jews.

1936 Attends International Writers' Conference in London. Lives
in Hampstead. Writes anti-Fascist poetry.

Hitler's troops march into the Rhineland and reclaim it for
Germany. A referendum on 29 March shows that 99% of
the German population supposedly approve of Hitler's policies.
German troops support Nationalist Forces in the Spanish Civil
War. The Olympic Games are held in Berlin. In September a
series of economic reforms (Four-Year Plan) is proclaimed.

1937 Begins work on *Fear and Misery of the Third Reich*.
Completes the Spanish play *Señora Carrar's Rifles*. Attends
International Writers' Conference in Paris: main theme,
intellectuals' attitudes towards the Spanish Civil War. Brands
himself 'one of the cowards' for being too cautious to go to
Madrid himself. In Paris, the premiere of *Señora Carrar's Rifles*.

On 30 January, the Enabling Law is extended for four years.
In November, Hitler meets in secret with his military chiefs, and
reveals his aggressive territorial plans. Sino-Japanese War in East
Asia.

1938 *Fear and Misery of the Third Reich* is premiered in Paris,
entitled 99%, and stars Helene Weigel. In July, Brecht sends a
manuscript consisting of twenty-seven scenes to his friend
Wieland Herzfelde of the Malik publishing house in Prague.
First version of *Life of Galileo* completed.

Hitler takes over supreme command of the armed forces. On
12–13 March, German troops enter Austria and 'annexe' it.
The country becomes a territory of the German Reich. Jews are

attacked across Germany on 8–9 November ('The Night of Broken Glass').

1939 Works by Brecht in Czechoslovakia are confiscated and pulped. Moves to Stockholm with his family. Not allowed to participate in political activities but continues under pseudonym of John Kent. Finishes *Mother Courage and Her Children*. Publication of *Svendborger Gedichte*.

Czechoslovakia is occupied by German troops. Hitler–Stalin pact. In September, Germany invades Poland. France and Britain declare war on Germany.

1940 Moves with family to Helsinki. Waits for visas to go to America.

Winston Churchill becomes British Prime Minister. Soviet Union occupies the Baltic states. Denmark and Norway occupied by German troops. Holland, Belgium, Luxembourg and France are invaded. Italy joins the war. France surrenders.

1941 Completes *The Good Person of Szechwan*, *Mr Puntila and his Man Matti* and *The Resistible Rise of Arturo Ui*. Writes war poetry and 'Finnish Epigrams'. Goes to the USA, via Leningrad, Moscow and Vladivostok, and settles in Santa Monica.

Attack on Pearl Harbor. United States enters the war. Battle of Britain. German armies invade the Soviet Union (Operation Barbarossa), Yugoslavia and Greece. Jews in Germany must wear the yellow Star of David and are prohibited from emigrating.

1942 Prepares *Poems in Exile* for publication. Two productions of selected scenes of *Fear and Misery of the Third Reich* in New York. Participates in anti-war, anti-Fascist activities of exile groups.

At the Wannsee Conference plans are finalised for the genocide of the European Jews. Beginning of mass gassings at Auschwitz.

1943   First performances of *Life of Galileo* and *The Good Person of Szechwan* in Zurich.

German troops surrender at Stalingrad. Allied offensives gain momentum.

1944   Eric Bentley and Elisabeth Hauptmann's English version of *Fear and Misery of the Third Reich*, *The Private Life of the Master Race*, published in America. Seventeen scenes, all chosen by Brecht. First version of *The Caucasian Chalk Circle*.

The Allied Forces invade northern France. Count Stauffenberg attempts to assassinate Hitler. The Red Army drives the Germans out of the Caucasus. Western Allies invade France; Paris liberated. Germany invaded from east and west.

1945   German version of *Fear and Misery of the Third Reich* published in New York: twenty-four scenes, compiled by Brecht. English productions at the University of California at Berkeley and in New York.

The fall of Berlin. 30 April Hitler commits suicide. 8 May the German surrender is signed. Potsdam Conference on the future of Europe. United States drops atomic bombs on Hiroshima and Nagasaki. Japan surrenders.

1946   Writes new final scene, 'Hamburg 1938', for first Swiss performance in Basel.

Germany governed by occupying forces in four territories: American, British, French and Russian.

1947   Charles Laughton appears in *Life of Galileo* in Beverly Hills and New York. Brecht is summoned before 'House Committee on Un-American Activities', proves himself master of ambiguity when cross-examined about his Communist sympathies. Brecht and Weigel go to Zurich.

Effective recognition of the two zones (Soviet and Western) in Germany.

1948 Publishes *Little Organum for the Theatre*. Swiss productions of *The Antigone of Sophocles* and *Mr Puntila*. Travels to Berlin.

The Berlin blockade.

1949 *Mother Courage* opens at Deutsches Theater in Soviet sector of Berlin. Brecht settles in Berlin and forms Berliner Ensemble, his and Weigel's own state-subsidised company. Opens with *Mr Puntila*.

Foundation of the Federal Republic of Germany and the German Democratic Republic.

1950 *The Tutor* performed at Berliner Ensemble, and *Mother Courage* in Zurich.

1951 *The Mother* performed at Berliner Ensemble, and a new production of *Mother Courage*.

1953 Brecht angry that a doctored version of a letter he wrote is published, making it seem that he sympathised with the forcible suppression of the workers' uprising on 17 June.

17 June strikes and demonstrations protesting about working conditions in the German Democratic Republic are suppressed by force.

1954 Berliner Ensemble acquires its own home at Theater am Schiffbauerdamm. Productions of *The Caucasian Chalk Circle* and *Mother Courage* (also on tour).

1955 Brecht travels to Moscow to receive Stalin Peace Prize.

1956 14 August Brecht dies of a heart attack.

1957 Studio performance of *Fear and Misery of the Third Reich* at Berliner Ensemble: ten scenes chosen by Brecht and Weigel.

Commentary

Bertolt Brecht is a giant in twentieth-century theatre, not just a great dramatist, but also one of the truly innovative thinkers and theorists. With Samuel Beckett, whose writing and ideas take us in a rather different direction, he transformed the modern scene. Beckett created a literature of stark and existential claims, which confronted the awful realities of the world in hard-edged and yet playful defiance. His literature plays itself out at the very edge of meaning. Brecht, on the other hand, was deeply embedded in the political realities of his time. He could not risk play or nonsense, and he had a deep mistrust of metaphysics. His literature is all about the material realities of this world, and he is not frightened to propose political solutions and directions. It is this that has made the reception of his work so fraught. For a start, his plays are sometimes seen as having validity only for the particular historical and political situations in which they were written. And then there is his allegiance to Communism. Although Brecht was never a member of the Party, it was clear that, from the age of about thirty, he was a dissident but committed Marxist. The decline of that world-view and the defeat of Communism in Europe, at least for the time being, have once again made it easy to dismiss Brecht's contribution, as only of 'historical' significance. Yet if there is one thing that Marx, and Brecht for that matter, teach us, it is that history is always also about the present: it provides us with a fund of analogies by which to understand our own world, it shows us where that world has come from, and, since the telling of history always contains also our own point of view, it gives us more tools by which to analyse our own assumptions and the forces which structure our present worlds. More than all of that, the study of history and of its relationship with the present also teaches us about historical change, about how conditions can be overcome: for a Marxist, history is a tool in the struggle. As we shall see, Brecht even equated 'historicisation' with his most famous theoretical term *Verfremdung* (usually translated as 'alienation') – this was a technique which was supposed to help us see beyond surface reality and our commonplace understandings, to help us analyse our world and show us how conditions could be overcome. If Brecht's writings are 'historical' in this sense, rather than merely in the sense of being dustily archival, then so be it.

The play that we are presenting in these pages is one of Brecht's most obviously historical and political. It is a play 'about' the Third Reich, as its title already tells us. And yet even this play, which, as we shall learn, was indubitably created to cater for a real political need and situation in the 1930s, has had a rich life since the defeat of Nazism. It is still often performed, and not merely as a history lesson – although it may be a good opportunity for that too. Its scenes have provided the inspiration and model for many other works of socially critical theatre.

Brecht's life

From Augsburg to Berlin
Brecht's own life coincided with the violence and turbulence of both the First and Second World Wars, and stretched from the last years of the Kaisers, through the Weimar Republic (as we have come to know the period after the First World War) and the National Socialist (Nazi) period, to the Europe of the Cold War and the founding years of the German Democratic Republic.

Born in Bavaria in 1898 to a prosperous family, Brecht quickly developed a serious ambition to learn the craft of the writer, which he practised in careful exercises and experiments in form. At the same time he had an irrepressibly rebellious streak, expressed in his first full-length play *Baal* and in numerous other sketches, songs and poems. Both the rebellion and the experimental approach were to remain central aspects of his career. Brecht's early literature is sometimes characterised as nihilistic, and certainly it seems to embrace a sort of chaotic iconoclasm, directed at prevailing standards of taste and morality. In one notebook from 1920 Brecht remarked, 'Values are in demand: I have a good sense of values (inheritance from my father). But I am also sensitive to the fact that one can set aside the concept of value altogether (Baal).'[1]

In 1914, at the outbreak of the First World War, Brecht was only sixteen. Like many other young men, he was initially caught up in the tide of militaristic enthusiasm which swept across Germany (and Europe). But before long there was a shift. Brecht became more and more conscientiously determined not to fulfil the expectations of his upbringing. Like many of his generation, he began to oppose the war, as a stupid gesture by the old bourgeois order of the doomed Wilhelmine Empire. He served briefly as a medical orderly in a hospital in his home-town, Augsburg. Then, in November 1918, a revolution was proclaimed in both Berlin and Munich, but Brecht seems to have been only marginally involved in all the politicking and excitement; he was more concerned with revising *Baal* and with the composition of his second play, *Drums in the Night*, in which the anti-hero proclaims at the end:

> The bagpipes play, the poor people are dying around the newspaper buildings, the houses fall on top of them, the dawn breaks, they lie like drowned kittens in the roadway, I'm a swine and the swine's going home.[2]

Not only was he determined to be anti-bourgeois and anti-patriotic, at this stage he was pretty determined not to commit

[1] Quoted in *Brecht on Art and Politics*, p. 10.
[2] *Collected Plays: 1*, p. 115.

himself to anything whatsoever. Yet this was the play for which Brecht won the coveted Kleist Prize in 1922, and which signalled a breakthrough to nationwide recognition.

Moving to Berlin, Brecht became something of a celebrity in the vibrant and avant-garde theatre scene, wrote more plays and poems, and acquired an interest in Communist politics and theory. It was in 1926 that he began to read Lenin and Marx and discovered interests in social conflict which chimed in with his own. He was to develop a close engagement with some of his more unorthodox Marxist contemporaries, most notably with the critic, commentator and philosopher Walter Benjamin, who became a good friend. It was not, however, the simple 'conversion' to Marxism that he himself would sometimes laconically describe, for example in the autobiographical poem 'Driven out with good reason': 'I left my own class and allied myself / With insignificant people.'[1]

The years from 1927 to 1933 constitute one of the most productive and problematic phases in Brecht's career. In this period he began to develop the ideas of epic theatre (see below) and a sophisticated theory of the role of art in society. He wrote a huge number of theoretical essays, both on the theatre specifically and also of more general cultural and social critique. His first major collection of poems, *The Domestic Breviary*, was published, and he composed, among several other dramatic works, the famous operas, *Mahagonny* and *The Threepenny Opera*, and the *Lehrstücke* (learning plays), collaborating with the composers, Kurt Weill and, then, hugely productively, Hanns Eisler. *The Threepenny Opera* was first performed in 1928, and was such a success that Brecht was now secure financially. From the very start, Brecht had liked to work collectively, collaborating with other artists and exploiting the talents even of his schoolfriends, one of whom, the graphic

[1] *Poems 1913–1956*, p. 317.

artist Caspar Neher, became his most trusted set-designer (he designed the first *Threepenny Opera*). Others, including a series of female partners – Elisabeth Hauptmann, Margarete Steffin and Ruth Berlau, as well as his second wife, Helene Weigel – collected material for his plays, typed his manuscripts, advised him and made their own contributions. Brecht mostly named these 'co-workers' in productions and publications, but their contribution has sometimes been obscured since. He also enjoyed an extremely fruitful association with the revolutionary political theatre director and theorist, Erwin Piscator. His work became explicitly Marxist and his writing paid increasing attention to the economic structures of capitalist society.

Exile

This fruitful and creative period was brutally interrupted by Nazism. In 1933, the day after the Reichstag Fire on 27 February, Brecht left Germany with his young family, at the beginning of what was to become a long exile. Of course, he had no idea how long it would be; with many, he hoped for an early overthrow of the Nazi regime. Circling Germany, he travelled via Austria, Switzerland and France, and settled first in Denmark, near the little town of Svendborg on the island of Fyn, just thirty miles across the sea from the northern coast of Germany. Opportunities for an involvement in the theatre here were few. Whereas before 1933 he could risk all sorts of experiments and might hope for multiple premieres in leading theatres and long runs, now the best he could aspire to was a few nights of an amateur production in some public hall. Cut off from German publics and publishers, he began to compile further collections of poems and, only hesitantly, started writing for the theatre again. It was in Svendborg that he wrote most of the scenes of *Fear and Misery of the Third Reich*. However, he travelled about a great deal throughout the 1930s, to

Moscow, Paris, London, among others: to promote his plays and organise productions, to participate in political events, to consider alternatives for himself and his family, and generally to maintain and establish contacts in the literary, cultural and political worlds. In all of these cities, as well as elsewhere, scenes from *Fear and Misery* were performed, published and broadcast, and the work swiftly established itself as the most widely distributed of all anti-Nazi works of theatre. Brecht's efforts were overwhelmingly directed at countering Nazism and fascism, at responding to the growing threat of war, and at engaging critically with the role of the Soviet Union. Peculiarly, given how little direct experience of the theatre he had in these years, he also continued and elaborated the theory of epic theatre.

In the autumn of 1939 war broke out and, as the German troops advanced through northern Europe, Brecht retreated, first to Sweden, then Finland. He continued writing. The European phase of his exile saw the composition of an important body of theoretical essays, the first anti-Nazi writings, satirical poems and plays, as well as *Mother Courage* and the first versions of *Life of Galileo* and *The Good Person of Szechwan*.

In 1941 Brecht crossed Stalin's Soviet Union by the trans-Siberian express, and, with his family, took a steamer to California. In the States he felt considerable alienation from his surroundings, and he found it hard to maintain and develop contacts. Nonetheless, he continued work on some of his most famous plays, including for example *The Caucasian Chalk Circle*. He tried to establish a foothold in Hollywood, and did some writing for the cinema (which had been an interest for a long time), but it did not come to much. He made contact with amateur and professional theatre people, notably the great Hollywood actor Charles Laughton, with whom he re-worked *Life of Galileo* into English and who played the lead role in a production in Beverly Hills and on Broadway. He tracked the progress of the war in Europe and the Middle and Far East, and compiled a vigorous anti-war critique of newspaper cuttings and short poems, called *The War Primer*. Remarkably, despite the obvious problems of being a writer and a dramatist in exile, it was in exile that Brecht developed perhaps his most characteristic voice and style, and wrote most of the works for which he is now famous. As he put it in one of the great poems from this period, 'To those born later':

> For we went, changing countries oftener than our shoes
> Through the wars of the classes, despairing
> When there was injustice only, and no rebellion.[1]

In 1943, listing all the plays he had completed over the previous ten years, Brecht was able to comment ruefully, 'not a bad repertoire for a defeated class'.[2]

The return to Europe

In 1947, immediately after a hearing at the McCarthyite 'House Un-American Activities Committee', which was charged with uncovering Communist elements in the Hollywood film industry, Brecht flew back to a devastated and divided Europe, in the first place to Switzerland, where he prepared a version of *Antigone* for the stage (again designed by Neher, who had stayed in Germany) and published his fullest statement of theatre theory, the *Short Organum on the Theatre*. After some negotiation, he and Helene Weigel were offered the opportunity to run their own theatre in East Berlin, the company that was to become the Berliner Ensemble. Here Brecht experienced the foundation of the German Democratic Republic and, having always been a profane and iconoclastic outsider, now had to negotiate a position as a foremost cultural representative, albeit a critical one, of the struggling

---

[1] *Poems 1913–1956*, p. 320.
[2] *Journals*, 21 July 1943.

republic. He devoted himself above all to the establishment of his theatre, to the publication of his own works, and to the training of a new generation of actors, writers and directors. He was a compulsive reviser of his own works, both in the light of changed political circumstances and in response to experience in the theatre. First versions were always provisional, so the plays that were now published or that came to production in Berlin and elsewhere were often rather different from the earlier versions. Nonetheless, in general it has been these later revised versions which have established themselves.

Brecht died, at a comparatively young age, in 1956, on the eve of the Berliner Ensemble's London tour. Weigel continued to run the Berliner Ensemble until her own death in 1971.

Brecht's politics and theory

The most commonplace misapprehension about Brecht's 'theory' is that there is some single body of doctrine about a simple set of concerns. There is not. A very large proportion of his writings is about the theatre, but even here his ideas are continually changing and shifting their ground and their emphases. To a certain extent we might wish to account for the variety and confusion by Brecht's personal intellectual habits: he had a lively, alert, sometimes slippery intellect, and he was sometimes maddeningly nonchalant about shifting his frame of reference; he did not set out to be a 'systematic thinker'. However, there are also essential reasons why Brecht's ideas might seem changeable, fragmentary, even contradictory. For a start, he soon decided that thought was not the 'property' of the individual, and argued that 'it is wrong to take a philosophy as the expression of a particular head, rather than as the play of the intellect itself'.[1] And increasingly he came

[1] *Brecht on Art and Politics*, p. 2.

to think of the divorce of theory from practice as a problem of 'bourgeois philosophy'; for him, theory was to be inseparable from practice, whether in the theatre or in political resistance to Nazism. For the modern Marxist, philosophy could not be simply a question of cooking up theories about a fixed object and an unchanging world. On the contrary, the ideas had to be able to intervene and participate in the reality (the fragmented, collectivist, late capitalist reality), just as the reality intervenes in the ideas. 'I wanted to take the principle that it was not just a matter of interpreting the world but of changing it, and apply that to the theatre.'[1] Both the theatre and the world had to be amenable to change. Indeed, 'change' and 'contradiction' become key categories in Brecht's thinking. This is at least one reason why his dramatic works often go through so many re-draftings and transformations.

As we have already seen, from an early age, and long before he became political, Brecht was inclined to rebel against conventions. There are perhaps two dominant strands of theatre in the early twentieth century against which he reacted. The first was Naturalism, the sort of theatre developed in Europe in the late nineteenth century and associated above all with Ibsen. This was a theatre that tried to give its audience 'a slice of life', the illusion of a real world on which the audience could eavesdrop and into which they could peek through the transparent 'fourth wall' between stage and auditorium. Brecht was consistently opposed to 'illusionism' and mostly scathing about the achievements of the Naturalists, even though they provided one of the obvious models of a socially engaged theatre. The second was Expressionism, the ecstatic and inward-looking movement that had developed before and during the First World War. For Brecht, the Expressionists were too emotional and too irrational. He reacted also against their

[1] *Brecht on Theatre*, p. 248. Brecht is taking up Marx's famous phrase, 'The philosophers so far have only interpreted the world; the point is to change it' (*Theses on Feuerbach*, 11).

individual and subjective takes on the world. Again, throughout his creative life, he remained mistrustful of excessive displays of emotion and strove for a more objective approach. This is true even of his earliest plays: they do not seek to create an image of the real world, rather they are conscious of their own theatricality; they do not wish to enthuse the audience, rather they ironise emotion and tease the public with controversial propositions.

When Brecht adopted and developed his own version of an unorthodox Marxism, his literature became increasingly motivated by the desire to analyse society, to attack social injustice and, tentatively, to propose alternative ways of organising social and economic life. His concept of the theatre too, above all at the time of the composition of the *Lehrstücke* (learning plays) around 1930, was driven by the desire, not just to present revolutionary ideas in the theatre, but to revolutionise the institution of the theatre itself, to make it more fit for political comment and critique, to enable it to reach a larger and more diverse public, and to reach that public intelligently. Brecht's theatre theory may grow out of a rejection of what others were doing, but it is also always itself a positive political undertaking.

It is also always quite consciously experimental. From 1930 Brecht started publishing his own works in little understated grey pamphlet volumes, that look for all the world like issues of some academic journal, entitled *Versuche* (Experiments). In these he published versions of his plays, poems, stories and theoretical essays alongside one another, without discriminating between the genres or between the literary and the 'non-literary'. The genres were permitted to rub shoulders and interact; the theory was to be a part of the practice and vice versa. Around the same time, theoretical essays started appearing in theatre programmes and the like, not just as an explanation, but rather as a polemical intervention to induce the public to see his theatre as something different. Brecht's theory was for the most part very practical. We need to understand it, but we also need to bear Brecht's ultimate objectives in mind. He wanted to create entertaining *and* politically instructive theatre. All the gestures and devices which we know as 'Brechtian' are efforts experimentally to transform the way in which audiences respond to a staged narrative, in order to influence and change interpretations of the world, and so – ultimately – to change the world itself. As the chorus of one of his learning plays, *The Decision* (1930), chants, 'Change the world, it needs it!'

The epic

In classical literary criticism, such as Aristotle is reputed to have taught in the fourth century BCE and such as Brecht learnt at school, there are three 'modes' of literature, or three larger genres which are held to contain all the smaller types and categories: the lyric, the epic and the dramatic. The lyric, which does not really concern us here, is taken to be the more or less unmediated expression of the thoughts and emotions of the poet, as if speaking directly to us. Its proper form is of course lyric poetry. The dramatic is more or less the opposite: the voice of the poet is now apparently absent from his own creation, and instead we witness, as it were from outside, the enactment of events in the lives of others, who speak their own words (the theatrical characters). For the home of the dramatic is of course the theatre. In between these two comes the epic. For Aristotle, this was the genre of epic poems such as the *Odyssey*, but more recent critics normally identify the novel as the realisation of the epic in the modern world. In this mode, although we are led through a plot as in a play, the scope is wider (the passage of time longer, the strands of causality more interwoven) and, above all, the events are narrated from a point of view, so that, one might say, we hear what seems to be the voice of the poet/novelist: in a framework, in a style or tone of voice, in interjections and instructions made directly to the reader. For example, in an epic ballad, it is this narrative voice that introduces the subject ('I'll tell you the tale of such-and-such ...') and that draws out any moral at the end.

To some extent, we can see that Brecht is being provocative when he puts the terms 'epic' and 'theatre' next to each other (although he was by no means the first to mix these mega-genres). More important than the provocation, however, is precisely this idea of introducing a narrative voice into the theatre. For Brecht, the events of the theatre were not supposed to be an enactment which we, as audience, happen to witness; rather, he wanted us to feel and realise that stories told in the theatre are also told from a point of view and for a purpose. To this end he often furnishes his plays with prologues (*The Caucasian Chalk Circle*), epilogues (*The Good Person of Szechwan*), introductions and frameworks (*Fear and Misery of the Third Reich*). Even as early as his *Man equals Man* (early 1920s) Brecht introduced an 'interlude' (which later became a prologue) in which one character, Widow Begbick, sings:

> Herr Bertolt Brecht maintains man equals man
> – A view that's been around since time began.
> But then Herr Brecht points out how far one can
> Manoeuvre and manipulate that man.
> Tonight you're going to see a man reassembled like a car
> Leaving all his individual components just as they are.[1]

The introduction of the name of the playwright, the anticipation of the argument, even the reference to the event in the theatre ('tonight') – all these things contribute to the 'epic' sense that this is a story being told to us for a purpose, not just an action that we relive. The quasi-experimental stance – 'let's tell this story and see what happens', 'let's try out this argument and see how you respond' – was also to become important for Brecht and a hallmark of his dramatic and theatrical practice, which sought to

[1] 'Interlude' between Scenes 8 and 9 of *Man equals Man, Collected Plays: 2*, p. 38.

engage the public, not just emotionally, but also intellectually. A much later but equally obvious example is the role of the 'Singer' in *The Caucasian Chalk Circle* (1944). He introduces the play-within-a-play, is onstage throughout, and not infrequently intervenes to comment on the action or to help it along. In *Fear and Misery* (1937/38) there are prefatory poems before each scene, and for the stage Brecht toyed with other frameworks too (see below).

So 'epic theatre' is at heart a simple idea, from which a great deal follows. Indeed, most of the things that we think of as 'Brechtian', the titles and anticipations of the action (the poems, and the dates and places in *Fear and Misery*), the direct addresses to the audience, the placards and the songs sung out of character as commentary on the action, the frequent changes of tone and switches of level, the theatre-within-the-theatre (the pantomime of 'The chalk cross', the 'rehearsals' of 'The Jewish wife', for example), the self-conscious insistence that we are, indeed, in a theatre (observing the scene changes and so on), and much of what later came to be called *Verfremdung*, can be understood as manifestations of this urge to create a theatre that is not so much 'dramatic' as 'epic'. Of course, many of these devices had a long history: Brecht drew on Greek classical theatre, on Japanese theatre, on the European baroque and, above all, on Shakespeare and the English Elizabethan theatre. But the point is that, for Brecht, all these techniques are employed for the promotion of what he saw as a more intelligent, critical and political theatre.

This overt mediation of the story, Brecht believed, was bound to provoke a more reflective attitude in his spectators. What they see is no longer a straight imitation of a real action, in which they become emotionally involved to the exclusion of all other responses; it is rather a story they are being told and on which they are invited to reflect critically. Could it have been told differently? Could it have happened differently? These are questions which are often explicitly broached within Brecht's plays.

Epic theatre v. dramatic theatre

All of this is cast by Brecht as a concerted reaction against 'Aristotelian' or 'dramatic' theatre (by which he often just meant most of the theatre that had preceded him). For Aristotle (who, like Brecht, was in fact no dogmatic ideologue) dramatic form, or specifically tragedy, had as its object the purgation (catharsis) of the audience's emotions (of pity and fear), by a process of empathy with the characters. Brecht proposed replacing pity and fear with 'a desire for knowledge' and 'a readiness to help'. His audiences were by all means permitted to get involved and be moved by the dramatic action, but they were not to empathise to such an extent that they could see no alternatives. Aristotelian tragedy, he thought, induced a passivity which could only serve political conformism. We emerge from tragedy thinking, 'That is terrible, devastating, such is life, there is no way out'. Instead, Brecht wanted to create a pedagogic theatre which could help to install an informed and questioning public. We are supposed to come out of a Brecht play thinking, 'That was terrible, but is life really like that? We have seen a possible human response to a situation, but was it the necessary response? Indeed, was it a necessary situation? How could we envisage a different outcome?' And so on.[1] In *Fear and Misery*, such questions are implicit: what would follow from that final exclamation, 'NO!'?

From this it must be clear that Brecht's epic theatre is not opposed to emotion (although this remains a persistent misunderstanding). On the contrary, it is emotional sympathy that

---

[1] Brecht imagined his own version of such responses in an essay of 1936, *Brecht on Theatre*, p. 71.

motivates progressive political involvement to improve the plight of the poor in the first place. It is merely an excess of emotion, or the indulgence of emotion to the exclusion of intelligent reflection that Brecht wanted to avoid. Indeed, the abrupt alternation of emotional involvement and critical reflection becomes the most obvious characteristic of epic theatre. For example, *Fear and Misery* juxtaposes scenes of very different weight and seriousness. The two short scenes in the concentration camps, 'Peat-bog soldiers' (4) and 'Servants of the people' (5), both designed to highlight unexpected divisions and kinships among the persecuted and the persecutors, are followed by the lengthy but almost farcical unravelling of the judicial system, 'Judicial process' (6), which will deliver more victims to the camps. The sickening fear of 'Charity begins at home' (16) is followed by the curiously caricatural 'Two bakers' (17). And between each scene we are thrown back out of the action for the more distanced and generalising verse commentaries.

Brecht first wrote explicitly about the idea of epic theatre (which he was not the first to propound – he borrowed the term from Piscator) in 1930 in his 'Notes to the Opera *The Rise and Fall of the City of Mahagonny*', a text which was published in the programme to the first production of that work.[1] Here he set out the famous and often reproduced table, of which this is an abridged version:

---

[1] It is reproduced in *Brecht on Theatre* under the title 'The Modern Theatre is the Epic Theatre', pp. 33–42.

Dramatic theatre	Epic theatre
plot	narrative
implicates the spectator in a stage situation	turns the spectator into an observer, but
wears down the capacity for action	arouses his capacity for action
provides him with sensations	forces him to take decisions
experience	picture of the world
[...]	[...]
instinctive feelings are preserved	brought to the point of recognition
the spectator is in the thick of it, shares the experience	the spectator stands outside, studies
[...]	[...]
the human being is taken for granted	the human being is the object of enquiry
he is unalterable	he is alterable and able to alter
eyes on the finish	eyes on the course
one scene makes another	each scene for itself
growth	montage
linear development	in curves
[...]	[...]
man as a fixed point	man as a process
thought determines being	social being determines thought

Perhaps the most important thing about this table is a note that Brecht added insisting that it showed only 'shifts of accent' and not 'absolute antitheses'. In later years he was often to modify and tinker with these tabular oppositions and even to suggest that it had been a mistake to lay out his ideas like this at all.

So, for Brecht, conventional drama (from classical tragedy to his immediate contemporaries) tended to be illusionistic, irrational and emotional. He sometimes called it 'culinary' because it satisfied the senses, but not the mind. It also depended on a conception of the individual which Brecht held to be out-of-date and 'bourgeois', namely that idea of the dominant character whose thoughts and emotions determine his place and his actions in the world, who may evolve or grow (in an almost organic way), and who benefits or suffers according to his 'nature'. Tragedy is unthinkable without the notion of individual integrity and responsibility. And it is no accident that *Fear and Misery* does not give us the opportunity to follow the fates of important individuals, but concentrates rather on snapshots of the little people. Brecht's epic theatre was to show us small individuals as socially constructed (and therefore able to be reassembled, like Galy Gay in *Man equals Man* or split into their components, like Shen Teh/Shui Ta) and battered in the struggle with the great forces of the time: 'oil, inflation, war, social struggles, the family, religion, wheat, the meat market' and so on.[1] These, rather than the inner lives of individuals, were to be the grand subject-matters and complex causalities of the new 'epic theatre' and their analysis justified his proclamation of a 'theatre for the scientific age'.

Verfremdung

Of all the terms which Brecht employed this was at the time perhaps the most important, and it has since become the notion which for most people defines Brechtian epic theatre. It has been variously translated, most commonly as 'alienation', but also 'defamiliarisation', 'estrangement' and others. It is probably best left as a German technical term; it is essentially Brecht's neologism, and we must accept that he wanted it to mean something more than any of the terms already in existence. *Verfremdung* enters Brecht's vocabulary in the early or mid-1930s, and he first

[1] *Brecht on Theatre*, p. 71.

published something using the word (about Chinese acting techniques) in 1936. We should beware of any over-precise dating, or indeed of any simple derivation: it is not at all clear that it is a translation of a Russian formalist term, 'ostranenie', or that it has anything to do with Marxist alienation (*Entfremdung*). The latter refers to the unworthy social conditions under capitalism. The former is a version (as Brecht's *Verfremdung* might also be) of the kind of productive defamiliarisation – a 'making strange' which enables us to see things afresh – which is widespread in art theory.

Brecht is certainly interested in enabling us to see things afresh, but there seems also to be, from the outset, a rather different and political component to his *Verfremdung*. In 1939 Brecht wrote, 'To subject an event or character to *Verfremdung* means, first of all, divesting the event or character of everything self-evident, familiar and apparently obvious and, instead, provoking astonishment and curiosity about them.' That much is easy to understand. But then he goes on: '*Verfremdung* thus implies historicisation, it means representing events and people as historical, and so as transitory. Of course you can do the same thing with contemporaries, their attitudes too can be presented as "of their time", historical, transitory.'[1] And a decade later: 'A true, profound and interventionist use of *Verfremdung* presupposes a society that understands its circumstances as historical and capable of improvement. The true V-effects are marked by the struggle.'[2] It is clear that astonishment and curiosity are not enough. It is no longer just a question of separating the experience of the audience (and the actors) from that of the theatrical characters; rather, it is an attempt to make productive that sensation of surprise, dismay, perhaps discomfort, which follows from jolting the audience's unexamined assumptions about their history, about their own

---

[1] 'On experimental theatre', *BFA* 22, pp. 554–5.
[2] *A Short Organum for the Theatre*, from the appendices not reproduced in *Brecht on Theatre*, *BFA* 23, p. 294.

society, and about art. Brecht had of course very urgent reason to want to see the conditions of Nazism as transitory and capable of being overcome. But in this theory, nothing is allowed any longer to seem firm or to be taken for granted, it may all be swept away in the tide of historical change. Brecht had little time for 'eternal verities'. On the contrary, the values in which we invest may also, in this sense, be made to seem historical, quaint and old-fashioned, as we re-examine, modify, discard them. *Verfremdung* is the process, as Brecht said elsewhere about realism, of 'laying bare society's causal nexus'. It is not just laying bare the artistic device (the theatre self-consciously revealing its own tricks); on the contrary, *Verfremdung* amounts to seeing through, not just the device, but, way beyond that, the customs and habits of mind which constitute ideology. All that we take for granted we have been, by a complex social process, conditioned to take for granted. We need to see that. There is always this social dimension. 'What is obvious is in a certain sense made incomprehensible, but this is only in order that it may then be made all the easier to comprehend.'[1]

If all that seems somewhat abstract, one might also say, simply, that *Verfremdung* is the term for the mobilisation of all those effects which we know as Brechtian and which help to deliver 'epic theatre', for the devices which Brecht uses to make sure that we can never identify too thoroughly with his characters, never get emotionally swept up by the action, and always see through to some sort of analysis. Such devices may include the purely textual – the odd and historically or geographically remote settings, the songs, and the addresses to the audience and so on – but they also include aspects of production and acting technique to which we shall return below – the revealing half-curtain, the few emblematic props and all the things that remind us we are in the theatre, the

[1] *Brecht on Theatre*, p. 78.

use of projected commentaries and placards, the masks, the music, and an acting style which was meant once more, not naturalistically to 'embody' character, but, by a sort of distanced stylisation, to reveal what it is that structures the social persona.

Despite its more 'realistic' appearance, *Fear and Misery* gives us examples of many of these sorts of technique. The ultimate purpose is to enable us to see through what on the surface may appear overwhelming and irresistible, namely triumphant Fascism, and to recognise its talk of heroes in fact as a strange outgrowth of bourgeois ideology and its economics as a perverse extension of class politics, all very definitely vulnerable to resistance and overthrow.

Other Brecht terms
There are several other words and phrases with special meanings, which are frequently employed in discussions of Brechtian theatre and which he used himself in his theoretical writings. Here are four of the most important:

Gestus: This is the most slippery of all of Brecht's terms (sometimes translated as 'gest', but the German/Latin is perhaps preferable). It comes into Brecht's specialist vocabulary from around 1929, initially in discussions with Kurt Weill, who talked about 'gestische Musik' (gestic music). Whereas we tend to think of a 'gesture' as making visible or underlining a thought, a feeling or an attitude, for Brecht a *Gestus* becomes, not the expression of a psychological event, but rather the manifestation of an external, social reality. So *Gestus* in the theatre is not subjective gesture, but rather a visible product of the social relations between people. The point is that we, as spectators, should be able to 'read' the movements Brecht's figures make on stage as revelatory in that social sense. For example, in 'The Jewish wife', when her husband passes Judith Keith her fur coat with the laconic last words of that scene, and she, despite her previous rehearsals, says nothing, we glimpse a whole world of social betrayal. Brecht is very sparing with his stage directions, but there are countless examples of revealing moments like this. Indeed, *Gestus* is a word very closely associated with *Fear and Misery*, which Brecht even referred to in his *Journals* as 'a catalogue of *Gestus* ... Gestics in a dictatorship' (15 August 1938). On other occasions Brecht talks also of 'gestic language' (apparently language that, as it were inadvertently, reveals underlying social relations). Elsewhere he expands the term to mean something like the 'thrust' or 'gist' or 'key moment' of a whole sequence or scene, again in the sense that it permits social analysis. This last meaning is the sense in which the term is most commonly used by English commentators on Brecht.

Separation of the elements: The first statement of epic theatre was in the programme for an opera, *The Rise and Fall of the City of Mahagonny*. Here Brecht was concerned to counter the Wagnerian idea of the *Gesamtkunstwerk*, the total, unified work of art, in which all the elements (music, text, stage design, etc.) would harmonise and reinforce one another. In Brecht's work, so he maintained, these elements should be kept separate, they should be allowed to contradict or furnish a sort of critical commentary on each other. The idea is of a productive and thought-provoking clash, rather than harmonisation – a harmonisation which Brecht anyway thought was forced or mendacious. If we listen to the musical settings of Brecht's favourite musical collaborator, Hanns Eisler, then we get some inkling of what he meant. In relation to stage action and *Gestus*, we might say that there is a greater potential for understanding and for getting beneath the surface of things if we can see a contradiction between what a figure says (or how it is said) and how he or she behaves or moves, and maybe even a further discrepancy between both of these and the setting in which the action takes place.

Montage: In the visual arts the word really means putting disparate found elements (cut-out fragments and illustrations) side by side and seeing what happens, in a somewhat uncontrolled way, as opposed to building a careful picture of organically linked pieces. We have already seen that, for Brecht, 'dramatic theatre' was a closed system of interdependent scenes, each one evolving inexorably from its predecessor, but with the plot so structured that the audience was kept in suspense, wondering how it would all end. The epic theatre was to be assembled as a montage of more independent incidents which demonstrated a process taking place. Referring back to that table from the 'Notes to *Mahagonny*', it would move from scene to scene by unexpected leaps and juxtapositions, which would keep the audience alert to the way in which things were happening (rather than being so focused on the outcome), so that they would be able, indeed compelled to pass judgement. Brecht explicitly referred to *Fear and Misery* as a montage (*Journals*, 15 August 1938). Montage was a popular technique with other modernist artists, most notably the Soviet Russian film-maker Sergei Eisenstein, whom Brecht admired. In German, moreover, the word does not have only aesthetic connotations, but also – attractively for Brecht – associations with the world of engineering, where it can mean 'assembly/assemblage' (e.g. of a motor car on the conveyor belt).

Dialectics: Long before Marx (and Hegel), dialectics was the process of arriving at conclusions in philosophy, not by a linear logical process of deduction, but by the to-and-fro of opposing viewpoints. This in itself would already be attractive to Brecht. In course of time 'dialectic' came to refer to an argument the terms of which are in continuous movement and even internal contradiction.

It became intimately associated with Marxism which, in the Soviet Union, became officially known as 'dialectical materialism'. The fundamentals of dialectical thought are: that there may be a unity of opposites; that quantitative change leads to qualitative change; and that change negates what is changed, but that further change (negation) does not lead us back to where we began, but to further progressive development. Brecht was fond of these argumentative techniques and, as he became a Marxist, he had all the more reason to subscribe to dialectics. In later life he even moved away from calling his theatre 'epic', and preferred the term 'dialectical theatre'. In the *Short Organum for the Theatre* of 1948, his most comprehensive attempt retrospectively to propound his theatre theory, he wrote:

> The theatre of the scientific age can make dialectics a pleasure. The surprises of a development that progresses logically or by leaps, the instability of all the conditions, the wit of the contradictions, and so on, these are pleasures we take in the vitality of humankind, of things and of processes, and they intensify the art of life, as well as the enjoyment of life.
>
> All arts contribute to the greatest of all arts, the art of life.[1]

Much earlier he had appended a motto to his reflections in *The Threepenny Lawsuit* (1931): 'Contradictions are our hope!'[2]

Brecht in the theatre

Brecht's ideas were conceived, not at all as the abstract theorisation of some static phenomenon, but rather in reaction to his own experiences, in practice and in response to his own work in the real theatre. The ideas developed and changed as his writing developed in response to new situations and experiences.

[1] *BFA* 23, p. 290. From an appendix not included in the English translation.
[2] *Brecht on Theatre*, p. 47.

Nonetheless, there are some characteristic aspects which remain
more or less constant. Brecht was often involved in productions of
his own works, sometimes as director, but more often as advisor
and (occasionally unwelcome) directorial assistant, so we know
very well how he actually wanted his plays to look and work. He
worked closely with designers, composers and actors, often
conducting, or participating in, rehearsals.

In contrast with the Naturalist stage, which tended to be
cluttered with realistic detail, Brecht's opposition to illusionism
meant that he favoured relatively bare stages with just a few props,
and that those props in turn were expected to do a lot of work to
establish the setting. The cart that Mother Courage pulls, in the
play of that name, is one of the most famous examples. At the
same time, it was crucial to establish a relationship between
the world of the stage and reality (even if it was not one of
straightforward imitation) so that the little things that were to play
a role in the action were often very carefully chosen and designed,
even if the larger context might look more abstract and unrealistic.
The props were to refer us directly to a tangible reality, not to be
loosely symbolic.

Early on Brecht worked with his close friend, Caspar Neher, to
design a stage that did not seek to disguise itself as the real world.
One of the main devices of this was Neher's plain half-curtain
strung loosely across the stage between scenes, above which the
audience could see the scenery being changed, and even
occasionally the actors' heads. It became a trademark of Brecht's
theatre that the lighting rig and stage machinery were kept in view,
to remind the audience at all times that they were in the theatre.
To the same end, actors would often put on their make-up or get
into character in full view of the spectators.

At the same time, some parts of the play were presented as if on
a different 'level of reality' from the rest. Prologues and interludes
were often played in front of the curtain. For songs the lighting

was changed and the singer would step forward, sometimes even coming right out of character. Back projections showed films, images and photographs, or sometimes short texts, which were designed to provide background information, or to link stage events with reality, or to comment on the stage action from another perspective.

Brecht also sought out actors who could create some distance between themselves and the part they were playing. He was fond of comic actors, who are often inclined to establish a relationship with the audience, as it were over the heads of their characters. For example, he was a great admirer of Charlie Chaplin. He also had a lot of time for amateur actors, who are simply unable to create the illusion that they have 'become' the character. He specifically commented, for example, that *Fear and Misery* was written in such a way that it could be performed by amateur workers' theatre groups.[1] In course of time, as he gathered his own troupe of favoured performers around him, and above all towards the end of his life when he was building up his own company at the Berliner Ensemble, Brecht trained his actors not to immerse themselves in their parts, but to understand them and their role in the social situation depicted by the play. This does not mean that the actor does not think himself into his part, but it does mean that he is discouraged from becoming possessed by it. The task of a Brechtian actor is to understand and communicate, not to empathise and be transformed. Above all there are clear contrasts with the naturalistic approach developed by Constantin Stanislavski at the Moscow Art Theatre in the early twentieth century. Stanislavski encouraged his actors to 'live the part', and by a process of intense emotional identification to 'be' the character they were playing. It is an even more purely psychological, empathetic variant of this approach to performance that has since become

[1] *Collected Plays: 4*, p. 327.

known in the United States as 'method acting'. Brecht utterly rejected this in favour of what he called 'epic acting' – showing, not being.

Although there is much emphasis nowadays, especially in Hollywood, on illusionistic realism, in fact many of the more superficial aspects of Brecht's theatre have become very familiar. Especially in 'art theatre' we are no longer in the least surprised if the stage is sparsely furnished, or we can see the lights or watch the actors put on their costumes. Sometimes one might even be seduced into believing that Brecht had won the arguments, and we were living with a post-Brechtian theatre. But this familiarity with anti-illusionistic devices can obscure the point that Brecht's underlying purpose was not merely another sort of entertainment, but a more thoughtful and socially critical theatre. That crucial social aspect can be just as absent from an anti-illusionist as from a naturalistic production.

Sometimes, perhaps because we can no longer appreciate so clearly what Brecht was reacting against in the theatre of his own time, and surely also because of common prejudice against the German and the Communist, people assume that Brecht's politics and theory must make his theatre into some deeply dull and ponderous tub-thumping. Nothing could be further from his purpose or his practice. Throughout his life, Brecht recognised and emphasised that theatre is, fundamentally, a form of entertainment. If you cannot delight the audience, and draw them into the experience, then there is no hope of slipping in some by-the-way enlightenment. Brecht's very last instructions, before he died in August 1956, to the members of the Berliner Ensemble as they planned their visit to London (with *Mother Courage*, *Trumpets and Drums*, and *The Caucasian Chalk Circle*) were posted on a noticeboard in the theatre: 'our playing must be quick, light and strong [...] we must think quickly as well [...] we must keep the pace of our run-throughs, but enriched with a gentle strength and our own enjoyment.'[1] Enjoyment is the key; and thinking, after all, 'is the most useful and pleasurable of activities'.[2]

Fear and Misery of the Third Reich: historical background

The so-called Third Reich was founded in 1933, when Adolf Hitler came to power as Chancellor of Germany. The 'first' and 'second' empires were the Holy Roman Empire of the German Nation (roughly 1000–1806 AD) and the unified German Empire respectively, the latter created in 1871 with Emperor Wilhelm I at its head and Otto von Bismarck as its Chancellor. By calling his state the 'Third Reich', Hitler asserted the novelty of the regime, affirming its difference from what had gone before, while simultaneously grounding it in history and tradition. The implicit link to the Holy Roman Empire allowed the Nazis to proclaim legitimacy and entitlement.

Hitler rose to power by exploiting the instability and insecurity of Germany during the 1920s, then a parliamentary democracy now known as the Weimar Republic. Following Germany's defeat in the First World War, the German empire collapsed and in 1919 a constitution was signed in the city of Weimar, establishing a parliamentary system which was then led by the centrist Social Democratic Party. The Republic, however, was blighted from the start, largely through the economic, military and territorial sanctions placed on Germany by the Versailles Peace Treaty (June 1919) that succeeded the First World War.

Hitler joined the German Workers' Party (DAP) in 1919, and gradually transformed it into the National Socialist German

[1] *Letters*, p. 562.
[2] The words of the old peasant Sen in Brecht's last completed play, *Turandot*, *Collected Plays: 8*, p. 189.

Workers' Party (NSDAP). Steadily gaining in popularity by playing on the German public's desire for national pride, a sense of belonging and of progress, the NSDAP reached a peak of electoral popularity in the parliamentary elections of July 1932, becoming the largest party in Germany. Thereafter, the party's popularity began to wane, and had the German President, former army general von Hindenburg, not attempted to prop up an ailing government by appointing Hitler as Chancellor in January 1933, the NSDAP might never have reached a position of supreme power. Similarly, if Germany's two left-wing parties, the Communist Party and the Socialist Party, had made the strategic decision to join forces in the last Weimar elections, their combined popular support would have defeated the Nazi Party. Nevertheless, Hitler was indeed handed the chancellorship on 30 January 1933, and began almost immediately to put in place a series of measures that limited the power of parliament and increased that of his government and of himself as Chancellor.

It is here, on the night of 30 January 1933 in Berlin, that *Fear and Misery of the Third Reich* begins, and over its five-year time-span it portrays the country's swift descent into dictatorship. By as early as November of that year, Germany was a one-party state, and in 1934 Hitler appointed himself President in addition to Chancellor. The anti-Semitic prejudice that was fundamental to Nazi identity was formalised in 1935, with the introduction of the so-called Nuremberg Race Laws, and the NSDAP's promise of territorial gains were first realised in 1936 with the re-occupation of the Rhineland, which had fallen under France's control after the First World War. Brecht's play ends where these expansionist aims become yet more palpable: with Germany's occupation of Austria in March 1938. The following year, the same treatment of Czechoslovakia and Poland propelled Europe into the Second World War.

Writing *Fear and Misery of the Third Reich*

Brecht began work on what became *Fear and Misery of the Third Reich* in 1937, although preparatory work was being carried out from 1933 onwards by his friend and collaborator Margarete Steffin, who collected newspaper articles and other documents of the effects of Nazi policy on the German population. These eyewitness reports fed into Brecht's composition of poetry during the mid-1930s, with poems including 'The neighbour' (1934), that forms a basis for the scene 'A case of betrayal', and 'The chalk cross' (1934), which contains the seeds of the scene of that name.[1]

According to his correspondence, Brecht began to write 'a series of short plays' in the summer of 1937, which by April 1938 he designated 'a series of horror-scenes'. The first playlets to be completed were 'The spy', 'The Jewish wife', 'Judicial process', 'The chalk cross' and 'Occupational disease', and these five scenes were collectively entitled 'Fear' and subtitled 'Spiritual Upsurge of the German People under the Nazi Regime'. Of these, 'The spy', 'The Jewish wife', 'Judicial process' and 'The chalk cross' came to be Brecht's core scenes, forming part of any production. By spring 1938 Brecht had written a further twelve scenes and the prologue, and he sent copies to the directors Slatan Dudow and Erwin Piscator, with whom he had previously worked in Berlin. This version formed the basis for the first production of the play, by Dudow in Paris on 21 and 22 May 1938, entitled 99% and set to music by Paul Dessau. The success of this performance fuelled Brecht's enthusiasm to publish the play, and increased his conviction that the text was an essential document of his position as exiled writer. In a letter at the end of May 1938 to his publisher, Wieland Herzfelde, Brecht insisted that the play be published together with his collection of 'Poems in Exile', which he

[1] *Poems 1913–1956*, p. 226 and *BFA* 14, p. 238.

claimed would make him the key figure of emigrant literature.[1] Some weeks later, Brecht sent a manuscript comprising twenty-seven scenes to Herzfelde, and suggested that the play be published under the title *Fear and Misery of the Third Reich*.[2] However, before this edition appeared, Herzfelde's press was taken over by the Nazis and the publication of Brecht's work banned. It was therefore not until the end of the Second World War, in 1945, that Brecht's play was finally published in its entirety. That year, the Aurora-Verlag published a full German text, which forms the twenty-four-scene basis for the present translation.

Fear

That Brecht considered fear to be the primary force driving the Third Reich is evident in his poem 'The Anxieties of the Regime', written at around the same time as *Fear and Misery of the Third Reich* (see Additional Texts). In this poem, a tourist who has recently returned from a visit to the Third Reich is asked who is in charge there, to which he replies: 'Fear'. This idea corresponds to the absence on stage of any leading Nazi figures. Rather, the play's focus rests on the impact that these figures, and their apparatus of terror, have on the German population. The fear and misery that they generate stand in for these leading figures, and their physical absence makes their power all the more haunting.

The title given, with Brecht's consent, to the English version of *Fear and Misery of the Third Reich* reflects more closely this focus on ordinary Germans: *The Private Life of the Master Race*. Other titles that were given to the play at different stages of its genesis were 99%, an ironic allusion to the percentage of the German population that allegedly supported Hitler's occupation of the

[1] *BFA* 29, p. 96.
[2] Ibid., p. 99.

Rhineland, according to a referendum in March 1936, and 'nineteenthirtyeight', the title that Brecht had in mind for a publication of the play with a selection of his exile poems. These titles reflect different aspects of the play, with the latter in particular emphasising the immediacy of its subject matter and underlining its documentary character. However, *Fear and Misery of the Third Reich* remained the play's principal and lasting title and it is indeed the most appropriate, for it is these two features of the Third Reich that define the entirety of the play's action.

Just as the play displays a panoramic vista of German society, so it portrays a range of different kinds of fear, emphasising the all-encompassing nature of the Nazi terror. Although the fear of persecution pervades the action, usually in the form of the terror exercised by the SA, SS and other Nazi functionaries, it is the less obvious forms of fear that have a more disturbing impact on the spectator. It is striking, for example, that the first scene does not portray fear of the SS, but rather the persecutors' fear of the persecuted. Set on the day of Hitler's accession to power, and therefore at a time when his followers should be feeling more secure than ever, the SS soldiers' crippling fear of the unknown other is represented. Having wandered into a part of Berlin that they do not know, the two soldiers fear for their own safety and so shoot indiscriminately at the slightest noise, indicative both of their own fear and of the irrational nature of Nazi fanaticism. The play thus makes a bold statement at its very opening: that the fear that defines the Third Reich is not only top-down, but envelops those who are themselves ostensibly in control.

This reversal of the expected order is extended to the ordinary German figures in the play, whose relationships are disrupted by the all-pervasive fear. Fear and distrust define the relationships between parents and children ('The spy', 'The Sermon on the Mount'), neighbours ('A case of betrayal'), old friends ('Release') and colleagues ('The physicists', 'Judicial process'). Significantly, these fears are rarely lent foundation by the action, but instead it is the fear itself that becomes the dominant motivating force. For example, although the audience is led to believe that the son in 'The spy' has not informed on his parents, nor has any intention of doing so, the parents' anxiety about the possibility of betrayal destroys their relationship anyway. Similarly, when a comrade is released from a concentration camp ('Release'), his neighbours can no longer trust him, for fear that he might have become an informer, which leaves their formerly close relationship in ruins. The spectre of betrayal, introduced in the second scene but thereafter not given such concrete form, thus haunts the entire play, more threatening precisely because of its enigmatic nature.

Deception and propaganda

So all-encompassing is the motif of fear that the play's other key concerns can all be characterised either as consequences or causes of that fear. The notion of deceit, for example, was considered by many of the play's first critics to be its dominant theme. One of the first to comment on the play was Brecht's friend, the German critic Walter Benjamin. Having read a manuscript of the play in 1938, he argued that each scene's principal concern was with deception, but ultimately related this to the dominance of fear, stating that 'the reign of terror [. . .] forces all human relations under the sway of deceit'.[1] In 1947 the Swiss playwright Max Frisch also argued that deception was at the core of the play, describing the text as depicting the 'birth of deceit', and emphasising its significance as a document that portrays the beginnings of the Nazi terror: 'We know the results, what we are looking for is the beginnings.' Similarly, the modern critic Franz Norbert Mennemeier asserted that the play's core theme was the

[1] *Brecht Handbuch* 1, p. 347.

status of deceit as both the means and the consequence of the Nazi terror.[1] Nevertheless, as Benjamin noted, throughout the play this key theme is subordinate to the principle of terror, which breeds such deceitfulness.

The additional concerns of propaganda and resistance are also intimately bound up with fear in the play. The issues of propaganda and press censorship arise frequently, either as the dominant theme of individual scenes or as asides, and thereby imply the extent to which this issue defined the experience of the Third Reich. The danger of listening to non-Nazi broadcasts is made plain in the second scene, 'A case of betrayal', when the couple's neighbour is arrested for listening to foreign broadcasts. In 'Workers' playtime', the broadcaster's careful re-interpretation of the factory workers' barbed comments displays the production of propaganda in action. Further, the lack of press freedom is implicit in the allusions to the Nazi daily newspaper, the *Völkischer Beobachter* ('The spy', 'Release'). Again, this issue is both a result and a consequence of fear: the Nazi authorities' fear of resistance, such that free speech is abolished; and the citizens' fear of reprisals if they allow themselves to speak freely or even to show an interest in unsanctioned media.

Resistance

The status of resistance in Brecht's play has been a constant source of debate within criticism. The overriding view has been that the play does not display convincing and active forms of resistance at work, but instead focuses rather on figures who either fail to resist altogether, or whose resistance is limited. If the play is viewed as a piece of propaganda itself, in that it represents an active engagement with the contemporary political situation and an

---

[1] *Brecht Handbuch* 1, p. 348.

attempt to galvanise resistance, then the lack of positive role
models does seem to be problematic. One of the first to voice this
criticism was the play's first director, Slatan Dudow. Brecht
fervently defended his text, arguing that resistance is at the core of
the play. He claimed that the scenes display a cross-section of all
classes and ranks of society, and that resistance is evident
throughout: 'resistance, yes, the increasing resistance of every
section of the population is shown clearly'.[1] However, the list of
examples that Brecht gives to support this point are in all but two
cases drawn from the working class (such as the factory workers in
'Workers' playtime') and petty-bourgeois characters (for example,
the shopkeepers in 'The old militant'). The exceptions are the
physicists, who resist by making use of Einstein's theories despite
his work being banned in the Third Reich, and the judge, who
resists – according to Brecht – by failing to pass judgement. These
characters are bourgeois intellectuals, and so do not fit into the
mould of working-class resistance that defines the rest of the play.

The levels of resistance shown in the play do therefore seem to
be linked to class issues. Scenes in which resistance appears to be
altogether absent include 'Occupational disease', 'The Jewish wife'
and 'The spy', and significantly the principal characters of these
scenes are all members of the professional bourgeoisie: doctors and
a teacher (the husband in 'The spy'). By contrast, the scenes that
do show limited amounts of resistance are peopled by members of
the working classes: factory workers in 'Workers' playtime';
peasant farmers in 'The farmer feeds his sow'; and tradesmen in
'Two bakers' and 'The old militant'. The only scene to show real
organised resistance is the final one, 'Consulting the people', in
which working-class members of a resistance cell discuss the
production of their next anti-Nazi pamphlet. The potential for
'secret, stubborn resistance', as critic and translator H.R. Hays put

---

[1] *Letters*, pp. 281–2.

it, is therefore in evidence primarily among the proletariat.[1]

Brecht's comments on resistance in his play shed light on his understanding of resistance itself. While he does see a role for organised resistance, as is exhibited in the final scene, he is more concerned with the part played by individuals in their cautious resistance to the Nazi hegemony. This resistance can take either a productive or destructive form, in that the individual either makes a gesture, perhaps clandestinely, that goes against state directives, or publicly rejects the status quo. The former position is exemplified by the farmer feeding his sow, despite state-issued instructions to the contrary, and by the baker refusing to adulterate his bread with bran. The latter is displayed by the old woman in Scene 16, who vomits the apple given to her by the SA men, and by the woman in 'Job creation', who refuses to keep quiet about the injustice of her brother's death. Brecht does not seem to differentiate between these two approaches, perceiving value in any act of dissidence, be it public or private. Indeed, the suicide of the 'old militant' in Scene 19 encapsulates both these forms of resistance: by killing himself, the butcher is enacting a form of individual resistance, yet by doing this publicly he turns it into a constructive act of overt resistance.

Brecht claimed that the emphasis on these wide-ranging forms of resistance would demonstrate 'too clearly what a fragile foundation fear and misery are for a Reich, how few supporters the Nazis can really count on, how ineffectual terror is bound to be, in fact, how inevitably it must create resistance, even in sections of the population that originally welcomed it with cheers'.[2] Although this focus on positive models of resistance is indeed one way of interpreting the play, a more pessimistic reading is still possible. While Brecht plays up the instances of solidarity between individuals, his scenes also exhibit how the mechanisms of the

---

[1] *Brecht Handbuch* 1, p. 347.
[2] *Letters*, p. 282.

Third Reich – and, perhaps, of any dictatorship – disrupt that solidarity between ordinary citizens, not only making successful resistance almost impossible but also irreparably damaging human relationships. The most prominent example of this issue is to be found in the second scene, 'A case of betrayal', for not only does neighbour betray neighbour, but the man and wife are no longer honest either with each other, or even with themselves. So while Brecht's portrayal of resistance may be class-oriented, his representation of the suffering caused by the Nazi dictatorship pays no heed to class divisions. No high-ranking Nazis figure among the characters, and all the others, whether worker, petty bourgeois or bourgeois, are portrayed as victims.

Realistic elements

Just as the term 'resistance' must be carefully defined when discussing *Fear and Misery of the Third Reich*, definitions are also at issue in a consideration of the dramaturgical features of the play. There has been much debate over the extent to which the play can be categorised as 'epic' or 'realistic', despite Brecht's own subtitle for the play: 'A piece of epic theatre'.[1] Several features seem to render the play more realistic than other examples of Brecht's epic theatre. Firstly, it is based substantially on eyewitness accounts and newspaper articles, and is set in the present day in a series of naturalistic settings that a contemporary audience would recognise from their own lives. Secondly, the dialogue is largely naturalistic, even making use of regional German dialects in Brecht's original version. Again, this kind of dialogue presents the audience with recognisable characters, increasing the likelihood of identification and indeed empathy. Thirdly, within individual scenes some of the characters are developed to the extent that their psychological

[1] *BFA* 24, p. 521.

motivation becomes apparent, which may further encourage a
spectator to engage emotionally with the character. Perhaps the
most poignant example of this exposition of psychological
motivation and process – what Brecht termed the display of
'intérieurs' – is in 'The Jewish wife'. Here, the wife's monologue
reveals her profound affection for her husband, through her
requests to friends and relatives to look after him, and her
readiness to put herself in danger and extreme discomfort in order
to protect him. At the same time, she expresses her disappointment
at the way in which the current political conditions have changed
her husband. Such a window on to the character's psyche might be
considered to go against the principles that define Brecht's epic
theatre, since they may lead the audience to identify emotionally
with the character. However, as will be seen, 'The Jewish wife' also
contains some of the most prominent examples of epic features in
the play.

Epic features

Walter Benjamin's interpretation of the dramaturgical features of
the play makes a useful distinction between its realistic and epic
features. He argues that, while each scene is based on the precepts
of traditional dramaturgy, by which he means Aristotle's definition
of theatre, the play as a whole is epic. Each scene does indeed
contain apparently realistic features, as detailed above, and in
addition obeys Artistotle's three unities: it is set in one place, over
a short and contained period of time, and follows one single line of
action. However, the structure of the play as a whole is decidedly
non-Aristotelian. The three unities are ignored, replaced by a
panoramic display of the German Reich across space (nineteen
different parts of the empire) and time (five years), while its
eighty-nine speaking parts people a series of entirely disconnected
plot-lines. Such breadth of focus renders the play 'epic' in a

common-parlance, pre-Brechtian sense of that term, in that it presents a vast array of characters and settings. This scope is underlined by the prologue, which foregrounds the whole play as a parody of a military parade, emphasising the scale of the project but also making ironic comment on the non-uniformity of the characters on the march.

The patchwork structure of the scene-cycle disrupts any suspense that might develop during individual scenes, and the interruptions of each scene-change further suspend the spectator's emotional involvement in the plot. Benjamin recognised this structure as an epic one and also aligned it with a filmic style, stating that epic theatre progressed in jolts, like films.[1] The scene titles and the verses that open each scene further augment this sense of dislocation, breaking up the action and reminding the audience that they are being shown a series of scenes rather than allowing them to become immersed in the story.

In a letter written in 1938, Brecht emphasised that he considered the play to be a whole cycle rather than a series of interchangeable scenes: 'I would rather not leave out a single scene, on the one hand in order to retain the play's integrity (and its continuity in the montage), on the other hand because, despite their brevity, these scenes portray certain attitudes that I required.'[2] This approach to the play's structure shows that Brecht viewed the play as epic. His use of the terms 'attitude' and 'portray' further compound this view, as one of the key features of epic acting for Brecht is that the actor should show a particular 'gestus' rather than act a fully rounded and believable character. In a note on this play, Brecht indeed describes it as a work that 'shows behaviour patterns typical of people of different classes under Fascist dictatorship, and not only the gestus of caution, self-protection, alarm and so forth but also that of resistance need to be brought

[1] *Brecht Handbuch* 1, p. 343.
[2] *BFA* 29, p. 98.

out'.[1] The short, self-contained, highly focused scenes bring each of these individual and specific gestus to the fore. The effect is therefore ultimately not Aristotelian, but epic.

The emphasis within the scenes on showing and on role-playing intensifies the play's epic features. For example, in 'The chalk cross' the worker succeeds in making dissident comments in front of the SA man, but only when he is called on to role-play the part of a subversive character. Similarly, the couple in 'The spy' attempt to act the role of good, obedient citizens of the Third Reich when they are in earshot of their maidservant, whose father is a local Nazi functionary. By the end of the scene, the audience is left with the impression that this role-playing may now be extended to their behaviour around their son, whom they suddenly suspect of being an informant. The scientists in 'The physicists', too, proclaim anti-Jewish prejudice in loud voices in order to be able to conduct their discussions about Einstein's theories in secret. Finally, 'The Jewish wife', discussed above in terms of its seemingly realistic and empathetic qualities, provides the basis for perhaps the most extended example of epic acting in the play. The female character is alone for most of the scene, making a series of telephone calls and then rehearsing her speech to her husband. Since the audience only hears one side of the calls, the scene essentially amounts to a series of monologues, which lend an artificiality to the action and thereby distance the audience from an empathetic engagement with the character. Further, the wife's rehearsal of her conversation with her husband throws into relief the fact that the play itself is simply a performance, and so compounds the spectator's alienation.

'The Jewish wife', then, functions as a paradigm of the whole play, in that it is constituted by a tension between realistic and epic features, between empathy and alienation. In his commentary on this play, Eric Bentley, Brecht's first American translator,

---

[1] *Collected Plays*: 4, p. 327.

celebrated this tension as a defining feature of Brecht's art. Describing 'the fine balance and interplay between *Einfühlung* [empathy] and *Verfremdung* [alienation] which Brecht's theatre aims at', he wrote:

> Aristotle said: pity *and* terror. Brecht says: sympathy *and* distance, attraction *and* repulsion, tenderness *and* horror. The tension of the two contrary impulses is the tension – so different from that of suspense – of the Brechtian theatre.[1]

Brecht, too, argued that the play is paradigmatic of the flexibility of his dramatic theory, in that *Fear and Misery of the Third Reich* demonstrates that 'both "intérieurs" and almost naturalistic elements' are within the range of epic theatre.[2]

A reading play

Fear and Misery of the Third Reich has regularly been criticised for its flatness when read, compared to the dynamism that can arise from a staging. Nevertheless, both Brecht and Benjamin considered it to be a text that is as worthy of reading as of staging, and seen from this angle its status as a kind of instruction manual becomes apparent. The structure of the play and the linguistic forms employed contribute to this effect. As a cycle of discrete scenes, depicting simple tableaux headed by either a straightforward label (such as 'The physicists') or an ironic label ('Occupational disease') and preceded by a succinct set of verses, the play resembles an instructive picture book, or a series of photographs with captions. A connection is thereby established to another of Brecht's works in exile, *War Primer*. Begun in 1940, this is a series of epigrams with photographs of scenes relating to the Second World War. The

[1] Eric Bentley, *The Brecht Commentaries*, p. 34.
[2] *Journals*, 15 August 1938, p. 13.

pithy phrases, proverbs and biblical sayings that litter *Fear and Misery of the Third Reich* anticipate the succinct epigrammatic texts of the *War Primer*, and also mirror the relationship between the words and the images in that later work. The scene titles and opening poems thus act like captions for pictures, instructing the reader or spectator on how the scene is to be interpreted.

Staging *Fear and Misery of the Third Reich*

In addition to its suitability for reading, Brecht considered *Fear and Misery of the Third Reich* to be easy to stage, and indeed he wished productions to remain uncomplicated. He intended it to be performed by small theatre groups, mainly groups of workers, and in a note on the play he emphasised its simplicity:

> Using simple indications of scenery (for instance, playing against dimly lit swastika flags), however, almost any theatre with a revolving or a multiple set could resolve the play's technical problems.[1]

Eric Bentley also underlined the simplicity of the production:

> The Brechtian theatre has few technical demands to make. It needs neither naturalistic paraphernalia nor expressionistic hocus-pocus. Readers of *The Private Life* will see that aside from one extraordinary item – the Panzer – the whole thing can be done with platforms, screens, and economical lighting.[2]

The structure of the play as a series of self-contained scenes further contributes to the ease of staging. While a complete production allows for the interplay and overlapping of scenes and contexts, it is possible for small theatre groups to construct shorter plays out of a limited number of scenes, rendering the play yet more

[1] *Collected Plays: 4*, p. 327.
[2] Bentley, *The Brecht Commentaries*, p. 32.

accessible, according to Brecht and Bentley, for exile theatre groups. Indeed, the play (or, at least, parts of it) became the most often performed of all anti-Nazi exile plays.

Despite its various on-stage manifestations, the play remains consistent in its influences. The montage structure championed by Brecht reflects common practices in film at the time. In particular, the very short scenes in the play, such as 'A case of betrayal' and 'Two bakers', are more suited to film than stage, because of the necessity for scene-changes in the theatre. Furthermore, by setting the play's framework during wartime, Brecht turns all of the play's main scenes into flashbacks, itself also a favoured filmic practice. The brevity of some of the scenes and the sudden black-outs and leaps from one tableau to another are also reminiscent of the cabaret, particularly popular in Berlin in the 1920s. Short scenes, often of a farcical nature (here, 'The physicists' particularly fits that mould), musical interludes and a comedic mode are all characteristic of the cabaret and all plentiful in *Fear and Misery of the Third Reich*.

However, the play by no means settles for the frivolity of a cabaret-style performance. Brecht skilfully combines this light-hearted structure with other practices more akin to the so-called Agitprop theatre of the Weimar Republic. This theatre, closely associated with the German Communist Party (KPD) and the Soviet bloc, was characterised by a documentary style, a non-linear structure and the insertion of songs. Short for Agitation-Propaganda theatre, these plays served to disseminate political ideas and to inspire their spectators to political action, which also chimes with Brecht's intentions for *Fear and Misery of the Third Reich*. So Brecht succeeds in combining this more serious aim with a comedic approach, thus producing a play that keeps empathy at a distance through humour and yet does not allow that humour to descend into triviality.

Humour in *Fear and Misery of the Third Reich*

The humour in the play arises primarily from irony and satire. The irony, often emphasised by the incongruous juxtaposition of scene title and action, underlines the disjuncture between the self-image of the regime and the reality on the ground. For example, the title of the fifth scene, 'Servants of the people', ironises the self-proclaimed image of the Nazi Party as serving the people, since the brief sketch shows the mindless brutality of the SS camp warders. The extreme negativity of the Nazi regime is thrown into relief by these incongruous juxtapositions. Other examples of such ironic scene titles are 'Charity begins at home', in which the so-called charity is revealed to be a mere mask for fear, intolerance and brutality; and 'Judicial process', since the notions of justice and method implied by that phrase are completely absent in the scene itself.

'Judicial process' also exemplifies Brecht's use of satire in the play. Typical of the structure of many of these scenes, the plot initially appears straightforward but gradually increases in complexity. In this case, that complexity contributes to the ridicule of the whole justice system, as the judge is rendered incapable of conducting the judicial process that is expected of him. Instead he is depicted being jostled from one layer of self-interest to another, unable to settle anywhere and therefore devoid of all the characteristics associated with the justice system. His increasing exasperation, the extreme complexity of the case and the sense of heightening tension as the court fills up and the temperature rises all contribute to Brecht's mockery of the judicial system. By probing one element of that system in intimate detail, taking the colossal machine apart and examining its components, Brecht exposes the absurdity of the regime in an attempt to undermine the threat that it represents. As Brecht himself argued, the laughter in the auditorium reflects the ridiculous nature of the Third Reich itself, and reveals the perpetrators for the cowards that they really are:

The spectators didn't seem in any way to share the horror of those on
stage, and as a result there was repeatedly laughter among the audience
without doing any damage to the profoundly serious character of the
performance. For this laughter seemed to apply to the stupidity that
found itself having to make use of force, and to the helplessness
that took the shape of brutality. Bullies were seen as men tripping over,
criminals as men who have made a mistake or allowed themselves to be
taken in.[1]

The tension indicated here by Brecht, between seriousness and
satire, defines the spectator's and reader's experience of the play as
a whole. Brecht's concern to express and display the extreme fear
and misery that he perceived at the core of the Nazi dictatorship
was deadly serious, but his method of revealing it fluctuates
between ridiculous exaggeration and incongruous understatement, as
a mode of articulating the absurd – and yet very real – nature of
the Nazi mechanisms of terror.

Fear and Misery of the Third Reich in the theatre

First performances
What was to become *Fear and Misery of the Third Reich* saw its
first production in Paris in May 1938, then entitled 99%. Brecht
provided eight scenes at the request of the director Slatan Dudow:
'The chalk cross', 'Judicial process', 'The Jewish wife', 'The spy',
'Charity begins at home', 'Two bakers', 'The farmer feeds his sow'
and 'Job creation'. Helene Weigel played the Jewish wife in this
performance, for the first of many productions, and the music for
piano and drums was composed by Paul Dessau. The German
critic Walter Benjamin wrote a review of this first performance, in
which he – among more positive comments about the structure of

---

[xx] 'The Augsburger's Theatre', *The Messingkauf Dialogues*, p. 72.

the play itself – criticised the performance of an actor who played an SA man with too much 'empathy'. He argued that such an approach was politically inappropriate, and so he implied that the epic mode of acting is an absolute necessity in this kind of role (quoted in *Brecht Handbuch* 1, p. 343).

The outbreak of the Second World War hindered any further European productions, and indeed the second time that the play was aired was in English on the radio. In fact, it appears that Brecht's original intention was for the playlets to be broadcast on the radio. During the 1930s Brecht worked closely with the 'Deutscher Freiheitssender' (German Freedom Station), the radio station of the exiled German Communist Party which broadcast from Spain during the Third Reich. He conceived his collection of poems known as 'German Satires' for radio broadcast, and his correspondence in 1937 suggests that he might initially have had the same aim in mind for the series of short plays that was to become *Fear and Misery of the Third Reich*.[1] The suitability of these plays for radio seems then to have been noted by the BBC, which broadcast selected scenes translated into English and entitled 'Under the Crooked Cross', on the Home and Overseas Service in December 1940, albeit with alterations and mistranslations that play down the Communist overtones of Brecht's version.

American productions

During this time Brecht had gone into exile in Scandinavia, waiting for his visa to emigrate to America. When he arrived there in 1941, his attentions turned to American performances and publications of his works, and it was consequently in America that the subsequent performances of *Fear and Misery of the Third Reich* were held, while Europe languished in the effects of the regime that Brecht

---

[1] *Letters*, p. 271.

had depicted in the play. In 1942, it seemed likely that the successful German émigré director Max Reinhardt would stage *Fear and Misery*, and as a result Brecht conceived a framework for the existing script. It seems that he recognised that as it stood the play functioned primarily as a text to be read (or to be broadcast on the radio) and that any staging would require a framework to bind the disparate scenes together. The new wartime context also demanded an updating of the play, to take account of the products of that regime fuelled by fear and misery.

In a letter informing the director Erwin Piscator of his plans for this play, Brecht had indicated that if a director wished to add any extra material between scenes, then it could be documentary, an innovation which would heighten the play's claims to immediacy and authenticity.[1] In the event, when Brecht conceived this framework for Reinhardt, he favoured the epic aspect of the work; and a connection was drawn between the original text and the war by depicting German soldiers on stage. A troop carrier rumbles on to the stage at the beginning and end, and twice during the play, and is full of actors playing soldiers with chalk-white faces, in order to exaggerate the fear that propels the action of the whole play. Further, the presence of soldiers on stage implies that all the persecuted individuals portrayed in the play's original scenes have now become Hitler's army. The truck is accompanied by the Horst-Wessel song, the anthem of the Nazi Party. These soldiers then act as the dramatic chorus, in the manner of a Greek tragedy, commenting on the action and so functioning as a bridge between the drama unfolding on stage and the audience. In addition, a lone voice speaks off stage between some of the scenes, performing the same function as the chorus but from a retrospective standpoint, explaining to the audience how each scene has demonstrated the development of one aspect of the Third Reich, from

---

[1] *Letters*, p. 280.

the betrayal of neighbour by neighbour (after Scene 2) to the oppression of peoples (before Scene 24). The epic mode of the play is emphasised by the instruction to hang banners above each scene detailing the time and place in which it is set.

In the event, a production by Reinhardt did not come to fruition, and instead the émigré Austrian director Berthold Viertel produced the play in May and June 1942 in New York, with a cast made up of similarly exiled German actors. The programme for this performance lists five scenes – 'The chalk cross', 'Judicial process', 'The Jewish wife', 'The spy' and 'The box'. Nevertheless, that last scene was ultimately not part of the production, so that this first performance consisted solely of the scenes that came to form the core of the play. Hermann Kesten, himself a German author living in America, wrote a muted review of this American premiere. He noted that the immense terror represented by the figure of Hitler lent itself more to literary comedy than to tragedy, and praised Brecht's play for its accessible humour.

The same year, 1942, saw two other manifestations of the play. Firstly, the Russian director Vsevolod Pudovkin created a film version, ominously entitled *The Murderers are on their Way*, which nevertheless was not released at the time owing to wartime licensing restrictions. Secondly, although Brecht did not know about it at the time, the scene 'The Jewish wife' was performed to Soviet soldiers on the Eastern Front in 1942 by the Russian actress Elena Kalatowa.

The English version, entitled *The Private Life of the Master Race* and comprising seventeen scenes chosen by Brecht and translated by Eric Bentley and Elisabeth Hauptmann, was published in America in 1944; while the German version of twenty-four scenes, which was entitled *Furcht und Elend des dritten Reiches* (*Fear and Misery of the Third Reich*) and is the basis for the present text, appeared in New York in 1945. When Erwin Piscator began to plan a production of *The Private Life of the Master Race* in New York in 1945, he added further to the framework provided by Brecht. The play would begin with actors and stagehands preparing the stage, thus heavy-handedly reminding the audience that they are watching a performance rather than allowing them to suspend their disbelief. Then an on-stage pianist would play the American national anthem, 'The Star-Spangled Banner', interrupted by a huge SS man with a revolver who would force him to switch to the Horst-Wessel song. This would be followed by a discussion about democracy and dictatorship (represented here by the American anthem and the Horst-Wessel song respectively), moving on to comments about the nature of epic theatre itself, before the troop-carrier would trundle on to begin the play proper. This version never made it to the stage, since Piscator abandoned his post as director days before the play opened, on the basis that he found Brecht impossible to work with. Berthold Viertel was brought in at the last minute to replace him, and the play was performed in June 1945 in New York, with music by Hanns Eisler.

This version consisted of nine scenes in English, including 'Peat-bog soldiers', which Brecht had written in 1942/43 in the United States. The set was created by images projected on to a screen at the back of the stage. Further, Brecht insisted that the face of the black narrator Maurice Ellis be painted white, an alienation effect that also referred to racial discrimination in America, which suggests that Brecht considered the play to have implications beyond the particular context of the Third Reich. Nevertheless, the reviews did not consider the play to have the same breadth of focus. Lewis Nichols, writing in the *New York Times*, described the play's message as already outdated, since the war was now over. Had it been put on two years previously, he reasoned, it would have made an important contribution to the struggle against Nazi ideology. In the post-war age, however, it was merely an interesting experiment.[1]

The same selection of scenes was performed that summer at the University of California at Berkeley, directed by Henry Schnitzler. A reviewer for the American magazine *Variety* was singly unimpressed by the play, complaining that it did not hold together and was unconvincing. The critic did praise the great comedy of 'Judicial process' and the wonderful irony of 'The spy', but ultimately found the unequal lengths of scenes and the colloquial style unsatisfactory. Judging the success of the play according to its commercial value, he concluded that it was worth 'nothing'.[2]

Post-war productions

The first post-war performance was given in Basel, Switzerland, in 1946. The processual and flexible nature of the play was reflected in Brecht's addition of a final scene for this production. Entitled 'Hamburg 1938', it is set in an impoverished flat where three SA men and a pregnant woman are listening to a militant Hitler speech on the radio. One of the men reads out a letter from a dissident, who is about to be executed, to his son – the same letter as in the final scene of the present edition, 'Consulting the people'. It is implied that the pregnant woman is moved by this letter, although the SA men insist that the man had it coming to him, a conviction that is confirmed by the final line of the scene (and therefore of the play): 'As the Führer says: In the end, it's the strongest who triumph.'[3]

Ernst Ginsberg directed a second production in Basel the following year, with the set designed by Brecht's great collaborator, Caspar Neher. In 1948, *Fear and Misery of the Third Reich* was

[1] James K. Lyon (ed.), *Brecht in den USA* (Frankfurt a. M., Suhrkamp, 1994), pp. 198–9.
[2] Ibid., pp. 188–9.
[3] *Collected Plays: 4*, p. 345.

performed for the first time on German soil, opening on
30 January in the Deutsches Theater in the Soviet sector of Berlin.
Directed by Wolfgang Langhoff and with set design by Werner Zipser,
the production was restricted owing to the material
hardship that prevailed in post-war Germany. The set was therefore
defined by highly primitive allusions: for example, in 'The spy' the
set comprised a simple wooden table and chairs, and a wooden
frame against a dark backdrop, which represented a door. The
following year, the play was produced once more in West
Germany, this time in Dortmund and directed by Herbert Junkers.
Here, all the action took place on a low podium positioned on the
black stage. At the side of the podium, two rows of plywood
figures formed a mute choir of SA men.

Fear and Misery of the Third Reich was not produced by the
Berliner Ensemble until after Brecht's death, in March 1957, and it
was therefore left up to Brecht's successors to direct it, with
Helene Weigel still playing the leading female roles. The cowering
figures on stage recalled, according to some critics, sketches by
the German artist and sculptor Käthe Kollwitz, whose
expressionistic etchings and woodcuts convey a profound empathy
with the victims of poverty, maltreatment and war. Others
highlighted the extent to which this production was a true
ensemble piece, with no one actor dominating the stage. Even
Helene Weigel, it seems, played a reserved 'Jewish wife', while her
strength came more to the fore when playing the role of a
worker's wife. Before each scene the context was brought into
sharp focus through multimedia effects. Scraps of film were
projected, such as glimpses of the erstwhile Nazi *Volksgerichtshof*
(People's Court), which had tried anti-Nazi political agitators.
Similarly, a recording of one of Hitler's speeches to the German
youth was played before 'The spy', in which a young boy's parents
suspect that he may denounce them as enemies of the regime.
These very concrete allusions were countered by the set, which was

sparse, and the harsh white lighting, which made the back of the stage fade from view, as if there were no back wall. Critics reviewing this production noted the similarities that it bore to the political 'Agitprop' theatre of the Soviet bloc (see p. lv). This Berliner Ensemble studio production of *Fear and Misery* saw 156 performances between 1957 and 1963.

Just as the text lends itself to ensemble acting, so one production of the play can be directed by several different directors, who may take a series of scenes each. This was often the case, such as for the Halberstadt production of November 1957, in which three directors produced a selection of scenes. The setting here was far from realistic, with merely one inner wall, a window with curtains drawn, a wall with tiles drawn on to represent a kitchen, and low walls as the embankment for the scene 'Peat-bog soldiers'.

Some years later, the play was put on in Ulm (March 1965). A reviewer for the *Schwäbische Zeitung* highlighted the restrained nature of the character portrayals, thus echoing the reception of the first Berliner Ensemble production:

> Valentin Jesker's production of the seven scenes was telling but restrained, without pathos, sentimentality or gimmicks. The immediately likeable ordinariness of the characters made the confusion of their thought and feeling all the more terrifying. Much was thereby gained for Brecht, if not perhaps all that might be.[1]

Adaptations

The post-war trajectory of the play confirms the text's extraordinary flexibility, in that it was employed both as anti-Fascist and anti-Communist propaganda. In 1959 the West Berliner Kabarett caused a furore by trying to re-name it *Fear and Misery of the Fourth Reich*, with 'The spy' referring to the surveillance

---

[1] H. Beil *et al.* (eds), *Bertolt Brecht on Stage.*

society in East Germany; and in 1985 there were eight productions
in East Germany, to celebrate the fortieth anniversary of the defeat
of Fascism. East German playwright Heiner Müller wrote an
'answer' to Brecht's play, a drama about the Third Reich entitled
The Battle: Scenes from Germany (written in 1951 but not
published until 1974). Müller attacked the myths about the Third
Reich that were being propagated in both East and West Germany,
challenging, for example, the heroic image of the Communist
resistance to Nazism, and questioning the widespread belief that
the German army had not committed any atrocities during the
Second World War. Franz Xaver Kroetz's drama about
unemployment, *Fear and Hope in Germany. A Play in 15 Scenes
from Everyday Life in Germany* (1984), is similarly based on
Brecht's play. *Fear and Misery of the Third Reich* has also inspired
plays about political concerns outside of Germany, in particular
political violence in Latin America, such as Griselda Gambaro's
play *Information for Foreigners* (Argentina, 1972) and Enrique
Buenaventura's *Documents from Hell* (Colombia, 1968). In English-
language drama, the American writer Tony Kushner's play *A
Bright Room Called Day* (1985) was also inspired by *Fear and
Misery of the Third Reich*. Set in Germany in the early 1930s and
with flash-forwards to Germany and America in the 1980s, the
play sets the rise of the Nazi party in Germany against the
increasing power of the Republican party in America during the
1980s.

Further Reading

Bertolt Brecht: *Brecht on Theatre*, ed. and trans. John Willett, Methuen, London, 1964; 2nd edn., 1974; and *Brecht on Art and Politics*, ed. Tom Kuhn and Steve Giles, Methuen, London, 2001. Brecht's essential theoretical and critical writings assembled in two handy volumes.

Brecht: Collected Plays (8 vols), Methuen Drama. All Brecht's own complete plays and one-acters in English translation. The volumes contain further contextual introductions, notes and other writings by Brecht relevant to each of the plays.

Brecht's *Diaries 1920–1922*, *Journals 1934–1955*, *Letters 1913–1956*, *Poems 1913–1956*, *Poems and Songs from the Plays*, *Short Stories 1921–1956*, *The Messingkauf Dialogues*, and *Brecht on Film and Radio*, all pub. Methuen Drama.

War Primer, Brecht's collection of press photographs and accompanying poems, pub. Libris, London.

Große kommentierte Berliner und Frankfurter Ausgabe, ed. Werner Hecht, Jan Knopf, Werner Mittenzwei *et al.*, in 30 vols, Aufbau, Berlin and Suhrkamp, Frankfurt a. M., 1987–2000 (BFA). The standard German edition.

Hermann Beil *et al.* (eds): *Bertolt Brecht on Stage*, Inter Nationes, Bad Godesberg, 1968. The catalogue for an exhibition on Brecht productions in West Germany. Includes details of individual productions, quotations from reviews and texts by Brecht, Teo Otto and Martin Esslin, all translated into English.

Eric Bentley: *The Brecht Commentaries, 1943–1980*, Methuen, London, 1981. Commentaries on Brecht's plays by one of his principal translators.

Keith A. Dickson: *Towards Utopia*, OUP, Oxford, 1978. Closely argued but accessible study of Brecht and his work. The book is organised around themes (Man and Society, The Historical Perspective, etc.) and deals with plays, poetry and prose.

Martin Esslin: *Brecht: A Choice of Evils*, Methuen, London, 1984 (originally 1959). An early and now dated study, the insights of which are marred by the author's antipathy to Brecht's politics. A historically important 'Cold War' reading.

Jan Knopf (ed.): *Brecht Handbuch in fünf Bänden*, vol. 1 *Stücke*, Metzler, Stuttgart and Weimar, 2001. Now established as the standard reference work in German, with essays on the genesis and textual history of each work, analyses in the light of previous criticism, etc.

Tom Kuhn and Karen Leeder (eds): *Empedocles' Shoe: Essays on Brecht's Poetry*, London, Methuen, 2002. Essays on some of the most important poems and collections, also assessing the legacy.

James K. Lyon: *Bertolt Brecht in America*, Methuen, London, 1982. A fascinating account of Brecht's US exile.

Siegfried Mews (ed.): *Critical Essays on Bertolt Brecht*, G.K. Hall, Boston MA, 1989. A compendium of essays (many of them historically important) by a wide range of authors – from Brecht's contemporaries to German, American and British critics of the 1970s and '80s. Essays on most of the major plays, as well on all sorts of other aspects.

Siegfried Mews (ed.): *A Bertolt Brecht Reference Companion*, Greenwood Press, Westport CT, 1997. Another collection, this time by an international team of modern critics, especially on aspects of theory, media and reception.

Michael Morley: *Brecht: A Study*, Heinemann, London, 1977. A brief survey of Brecht's work, including the poems, with the plays grouped in chapters according to theme or style.

Hanns Otto Münsterer: *The Young Brecht*, Libris, London, 1992.

An intriguing account of the first years of Brecht's creative career, written from personal memory.

Jan Needle and Peter Thomson: *Brecht*, Blackwell, Oxford, 1981. Useful on the plays in performance.

Ekkehard Schall: *The Craft of Theatre: Seminars and Discussions in Brechtian Theatre*, London, Methuen Drama, 2008. Accounts from personal experience by Brecht's son-in-law, a renowned Berliner Ensemble actor.

Ronald Speirs: *Bertolt Brecht*, Macmillan, Basingstoke, 1987. A very useful and accessible short introduction, with sections on most of the plays.

Peter Thomson and Glendyr Sacks (eds): *The Cambridge Companion to Brecht*, CUP, Cambridge, 1994: 2nd edn. (with new essays), 2006. A very mixed bag of essays by various authors. Good on theory, poetry, music, film and performance; the essays on the plays are often descriptive and from a 'theatre studies' perspective.

Stephen Unwin: *A Guide to the Plays of Bertolt Brecht*, Methuen, London, 2005. A collection of contextual chapters and plot summaries, introducing each play, with notes on the text in performance.

Klaus Völker: *Brecht Chronicle*, Seabury Press, New York, 1975. Detailed biography relating events in Brecht's personal, artistic and political life to his various writings.

John J. White: *Bertolt Brecht's Dramatic Theory*, Camden House, Rochester NY and Woodbridge, Suffolk, 2004. A dense and authoritative guide through Brecht's principal theoretical writings.

John Willett: *The Theatre of Bertolt Brecht*, Methuen, London, 1977 (originally 1959). Seminal but now dated compendium of basic information by Brecht's first major translator and editor in English.

John Willett: *Brecht in Context*, Methuen, London, 1984; rev. edn.

1998. Looks at Brecht from several aspects such as politics, music, Expressionism, etc. Includes impressions of Berliner Ensemble productions.

1. 'Judicial process', caricature by Heinz Lohmar for the programme of the Paris premiere in 1938 (under the title 99%). Lohmar was the set designer for that production; part of his design is visible in photograph 2.

2. 'Charity begins at home', a scene from the Paris premiere, with Helene Weigel, directed by Slatan Dudow, designed by Heinz Lohmar.

Der Entlassene

3. 'Release', one of a series of sketches by Brecht's favourite designer, Caspar Neher, created in the late 1940s but not used in a production.

4. 'Consulting the people', the final scene of the play in the
production at the Berliner Ensemble in 1957, with Helene Weigel,
directed by Peter Palitzsch.

Fear and Misery of the Third Reich

24 scenes

Collaborator: M. STEFFIN

Translator: JOHN WILLETT

Characters:

1 TWO SS OFFICERS
2 MAN
  WOMAN
3 SA MAN
  COOK
  MAIDSERVANT
  CHAUFFEUR
  WORKER
4 BRÜHL
  DIEVENBACH
  LOHMANN
  JEHOVAH'S WITNESS
  SS MAN
5 SS MAN
  DETAINEE
  SS OFFICER
6 JUDGE
  INSPECTOR
  PROSECUTOR
  USHER
  MAIDSERVANT
  SENIOR JUDGE
7 TWO PATIENTS
  SURGEON
  SISTER
  THREE ASSISTANTS
  NURSES
8 X AND Y, SCIENTISTS
9 WOMAN
  HUSBAND
10 MAIDSERVANT
  MAN
  WIFE
  BOY
11 DAUGHTER
  MOTHER
12 STUDENT
  YOUNG WORKER
  GROUP LEADER

13 ANNOUNCER
  TWO MALE WORKERS
  WOMAN WORKER
  GENTLEMAN
  SA MAN
14 WOMAN
  SA MEN
  CHILD
  WORKER
  YOUNG WOMAN
15 MAN
  WIFE
  RELEASED MAN
16 OLD WOMAN
  YOUNG WOMAN
  TWO SA MEN
17 TWO BAKERS
18 FARMER
  FARMER'S WIFE
19 PETIT-BOURGEOIS
  TWO WOMEN
  YOUNG FELLOW
  DAIRYWOMAN
  BUTCHER'S WIFE
20 DYING MAN
  WIFE
  SON
  PASTOR
21 FIVE BOYS
  SCHARFÜHRER
22 TWO BOYS
23 NEIGHBOUR
  MAN
  WIFE
24 WOMAN
  TWO WORKERS

THE GERMAN MARCH-PAST

When He had ruled five years, and they informed us
That He who claimed to have been sent by God
Was ready for His promised war, the steelworks
Had forged tank, gun and warship, and there waited
Within His hangers aircraft in so great a number
That they, leaving the earth at His command
Would darken all the heavens, then we became determined
To see what sort of nation, formed from what sort of
      people
In what condition, what sort of thoughts thinking
He would be calling to His colours. We staged a march-
      past.

See, now they come towards us
A motley sight rewards us
Their banners go before.
To show how straight their course is
They carry crooked crosses
Which double-cross the poor.

Some march along like dummies
Others crawl on their tummies
Towards the war He's planned.
One hears no lamentation
No murmurs of vexation
One only hears the band.

With wives and kids arriving
Five years they've been surviving.
Five more is more than they'll last.
A ramshackle collection
They parade for our inspection
As they come marching past.

One big family

First the SS approaches.
Blown up with beer and speeches
They're in a kind of daze.
Their aim is a People imperious
Respected and powerful and serious –
Above all, one that obeys.

The night of January 30th, 1933. Two SS officers lurching down the street.

THE FIRST: Top dogs, that's us. That torchlight procession, impressive, what? Broke one moment, next day running the government. Rags to riches in a single day.
They make water.

THE SECOND: And now it'll be a united nation. I'm expecting the German people to have an unprecedented moral revival.

THE FIRST: Wait till we've coaxed German Man out from among all those filthy subhumans. Hey, what part of Berlin is this? Not a flag showing.

THE SECOND: We've come the wrong way.

THE FIRST: A horrible sight.

THE SECOND: Lot of crooks round here.

THE FIRST: Think it could be dangerous?

THE SECOND: Decent comrades don't live in such slums.

THE FIRST: Not a light to be seen either.

THE SECOND: Nobody at home.

THE FIRST: That lot are. Catch them coming along to watch the birth of the Third Reich. We'd best cover our rear.
Staggering, they set off again, the first following the second.

THE FIRST: Isn't this the bit by the canal?

THE SECOND: Don't ask me.

THE FIRST: Over by the corner's where we cleaned up a bunch of Marxists. Afterwards they said it was a Catholic youth club. Pack of lies. Not one of them was wearing a collar.

THE SECOND: Think he'll really make us a united nation?

THE FIRST: He'll make anything.

He stops, freezes and listens. Somewhere a window has been opened.

THE SECOND: Wozzat?

He pushes forward the safety catch on his revolver. An old man in a nightshirt leans out of the window and is heard softly calling 'Emma, are you there?'

THE SECOND: That's them!

He rushes round like a maniac, and starts shooting in every direction.

THE FIRST *bellows*: Help!

Behind a window opposite the one where the old man is still standing a terrible cry is heard. Someone has been hit.

2

A case of betrayal

The next to appear are the traitors
Who've given away their neighbours.
They know that people know.
If only the street would forget them!
They could sleep if their conscience would let them
But there's so far still to go.

Breslau 1933. Lower-middle-class flat. A man and a woman are standing by the door listening. They are very pale.

THE WOMAN: They've got to the ground floor.

THE MAN: Not quite.

THE WOMAN: They've smashed the banisters. He'd already passed out when they dragged him out of his flat.

THE MAN: I simply said the sound of foreign broadcasts didn't come from here.

THE WOMAN: That wasn't all you said.

THE MAN: I said nothing more than that.

THE WOMAN: Don't look at me that way. If you said nothing more, then you said nothing more.

THE MAN: That's the point.

THE WOMAN: Why not go round to the police and make a statement saying nobody called there on Saturday?

Pause.

THE MAN: Catch me going to the police. It was inhuman, the way they were treating him.

THE WOMAN: He asked for it. What's he want to meddle in politics for?

THE MAN: They didn't have to rip his jacket though. Our sort isn't that well off for clothes.

THE WOMAN: What's a jacket more or less?

THE MAN: They didn't have to rip it.

3
The chalk cross

> Here come the brown storm troopers
> That keen-eyed squad of snoopers
> To check where each man stands
> Their job's to put the boot in
> Then hang around saluting
> With bloodstained empty hands.

Berlin 1933. Kitchen of a gentleman's house. The SA man, the cook, the maidservant, the chauffeur.

THE MAIDSERVANT: Did they really only give you half an hour off?

THE SA MAN: Night exercise.

THE COOK: What are all these exercises about?

THE SA MAN: That's an official secret.

THE COOK: Is there a raid on?

THE SA MAN: Like to know, wouldn't you? None of you is going to find out from me. Wild horses wouldn't drag it from me.

THE MAIDSERVANT: So you got to go all the way out to Reinickendorf?

THE SA MAN: Reinickendorf or Rummelsburg or might be Lichtenfelde, why not eh?

THE MAIDSERVANT *somewhat confused*: Won't you have a bit to eat before going off?

THE SA MAN: If you twist my arm. Bring on the field kitchen. *The cook brings in a tray.* No, you don't catch us talking. Always take the enemy by surprise. Zoom in from an unexpected direction. Look at the way the Führer prepares one of his coups. Like trying to see through a brick wall. No way of telling beforehand. For all I know he can't even tell himself. And then wham! – like that. It's amazing what happens. That's what makes people so frightened of us. *He has tucked in his napkin. With knife and fork poised he enquires*: How about if the gentry suddenly pop in, Anna? Me sitting here with a mouth full of sauce. *Exaggerating as though his mouth was full*: Heil Hitler!

THE MAIDSERVANT: Oh, they'll ring for the car first, won't they, Mr Francke?

THE CHAUFFEUR: What d'you say? Oh, of course.

Pacified, the SA man starts turning his attention to the tray.

THE MAIDSERVANT *sitting down beside him*: Don't you feel tired?

THE SA MAN: Bet your life.

THE MAIDSERVANT: But you've got Friday off, haven't you?

THE SA MAN *nods*: If nothing crops up.

THE MAIDSERVANT: Listen. Getting your watch mended was four marks fifty.

THE SA MAN: A bloody scandal.

THE MAIDSERVANT: The watch itself only cost 12 marks.

THE SA MAN: Is that assistant at the hardware shop still as saucy as ever?

THE MAIDSERVANT: Christ alive.

THE SA MAN: You only got to tell me.

THE MAIDSERVANT: I tell you everything anyway. Wearing your new boots are you?

THE SA MAN *not interested*: Yes, what about it?

THE MAIDSERVANT: Minna, you seen Theo's new boots yet?

THE COOK: No.

THE MAIDSERVANT: Let's have a look, then. That's what they're giving them now.

The SA man, his mouth full, stretches out his leg to be inspected.

Lovely, aren't they?

The SA man looks around, seeking something.

THE COOK: Something missing?

THE SA MAN: Bit dry here.

THE MAIDSERVANT: Like some beer, love? I'll get it.

She hurries out.

THE COOK: She'd run her legs off for you, Herr Theo.

THE SA MAN: Yeh, I always do okay. Wham, like that.

THE COOK: You men take a lot for granted, don't you?

THE SA MAN: That's what women want. *Seeing the cook lift a heavy pot.* What are you breaking your back for? Don't you bother, that's my job. *He carries the pot for her.*

THE COOK: That's real good of you. You're always finding things to do for me. Pity other people aren't so considerate. *With a look at the chauffeur.*

THE SA MAN: Don't have to make a song and dance of it. We're glad to help.

There's a knock at the kitchen door.

THE COOK: That'll be my brother. He's bringing a valve for the wireless. *She admits her brother, a worker.* My brother.

THE SA MAN *and* THE CHAUFFEUR: Heil Hitler!

The worker mumbles something that could be taken for 'Heil Hitler' at a pinch.

THE COOK: Got the valve, have you?

THE WORKER: Yes.

THE COOK: Want to put it in right away?

The two go out.

THE SA MAN: What's that fellow do?

THE CHAUFFEUR: Out of a job.

THE SA MAN: Come here often?

THE CHAUFFEUR *shrugging his shoulders*: I'm not here that much.

THE SA MAN: Anyhow the old girl's a hundred per cent for Germany.

THE CHAUFFEUR: You bet.

THE SA MAN: But that wouldn't stop her brother being something quite different.

THE CHAUFFEUR: Got any definite reason to suspect him?

THE SA MAN: Me? No. Never. I never suspect anyone. You suspect somebody, see, and it's the same as being sure, almost. And then the fur will fly.

THE CHAUFFEUR *murmurs*: Wham, like that.

THE SA MAN: That's right. *Leaning back, with one eye shut*: Could you understand what he was mumbling? *He imitates the worker's greeting*: Might have been 'Heil Hitler'. Might not. Me and that lot's old pals.

He gives a resounding laugh. The cook and the worker return. She sets food before him.

THE COOK: My brother's that clever with the wireless. And yet he doesn't care a bit about listening to it. If I'd the time I'd always be putting it on. *To the worker*: And you've got more time than you know what to do with, Franz.

THE SA MAN: What's that? Got a wireless and never puts the thing on?

THE WORKER: Bit of music sometimes.

THE COOK: And to think he made himself that smashing set out of twice nothing.

THE SA MAN: How many valves you got then?

THE WORKER *with a challenging stare*: Four.

THE SA MAN: Well, well, no accounting for taste. *To chauffeur*: Is there?

Maidservant comes back with the beer.

THE MAIDSERVANT: Ice cold.

THE SA MAN *putting his hand on hers in a friendly way*: You're puffed, girl. No call to rush like that, I wouldn't have minded waiting.

She pours the bottle out for him.

THE MAIDSERVANT: Doesn't matter. *Shakes hands with the*

worker: Did you bring the valve? Fancy walking all that way here. *To the SA man*: He lives out in Moabit.

THE SA MAN: Hey, where's my beer got to? Somebody's drunk my beer. *To the chauffeur*: Was it you drunk my beer?

THE CHAUFFEUR: No, certainly not. What d'you say that for? Has your beer gone?

THE MAIDSERVANT: But I poured it out for you.

THE SA MAN *to the cook*: You swigged my beer, you did. *Gives a resounding laugh.* Keep your hair on. Little trick they teach you in our squad. How to knock back a beer without being seen or heard. *To the worker*: Did you want to say something?

THE WORKER: That trick's got whiskers.

THE SA MAN: Let's see how you do it then. *He pours him a beer from the bottle.*

THE WORKER: Right. Here I have one beer. *He raises his glass.* And now for the trick. *Calmly and appreciatively he drinks the beer.*

THE COOK: But we all saw you.

THE WORKER *wiping his mouth*: Did you? Then I must have done it wrong.

The chauffeur laughs aloud.

THE SA MAN: What's so funny about that?

THE WORKER: You couldn't have done it any different. How did you do it, then?

THE SA MAN: How can I show you when you've drunk up all my beer?

THE WORKER: Of course. That's right. You can't do that trick without beer. D'you know another trick? You people surely know more than one trick.

THE SA MAN: What d'you mean, 'you people'?

THE WORKER: You young fellows.

THE SA MAN: Oh.

THE MAIDSERVANT: But Theo, Mr Lincke was only joking.

THE WORKER *thinks he had better be conciliatory*: Don't mind, do you?

THE COOK: I'll get you another beer.

THE SA MAN: No call for that. I washed my food down all right.

THE COOK: Herr Theo can take a joke.

THE SA MAN *to the worker*: Why not sit down? We won't bite your head off.

The worker sits down.

Live and let live. And a joke now and then. Why not? Public opinion, that's the one thing we're really strict about.

THE COOK: A good thing you are.

THE WORKER: And how's public opinion these days?

THE SA MAN: Public opinion these days is fine. You with me there?

THE WORKER: Oh yes. It's just that nobody tells anyone what he thinks.

THE SA MAN: Nobody tells anyone? What d'you mean? They tell me all right.

THE WORKER: Really?

THE SA MAN: Well of course they're not going to come along and tell you all their thoughts. You go to them.

THE WORKER: Where?

THE SA MAN: To the public welfare for instance. In the mornings we'll be at the public welfare.

THE WORKER: That's right, now and again you hear somebody grumbling there.

THE SA MAN: You see?

THE WORKER: But that way all you can do is catch them once, then they know you. And after that they'll clam up again.

THE SA MAN: Why should they know me? Shall I show you why they don't? Interested in tricks, aren't you? No reason why I shouldn't show you one, we've got plenty. I always say if they only realised what a lot we've got up our sleeve, and how they'll never survive whatever happens, then perhaps they'd pack it in.

THE MAIDSERVANT: Go on, Theo, tell them how you do it.

THE SA MAN: Right. Let's suppose we're at the public welfare in the Münzstrasse. Let's say you – *looking at the worker* – are in the line ahead of me. But I got to make a few preparations first. *He goes out.*

THE WORKER *winking at the chauffeur*: So now we're getting a chance to see how they do it.

THE COOK: They're going to smell out all the Marxists because they got to be stopped disrupting everything.

THE WORKER: Is that it?

The SA man comes back.

THE SA MAN: I'd be in civvies of course. *To the worker*: Okay, start grumbling.

THE WORKER: What about?

THE SA MAN: Go on, you've got something on your chest. Your lot always have.

THE WORKER: Me? No.

THE SA MAN: You're a tough guy, aren't you? Don't tell me you think everything's a hundred per cent.

THE WORKER: Why not?

THE SA MAN: All right, let's call it off. If you won't play the whole thing's off.

THE WORKER: All right then. I'll shoot my mouth off for you. These buggers keep you hanging about as if we'd all the time in the world. Two hours it took me to get here from Rummelsburg.

THE SA MAN: What the hell. Don't tell me the distance from Rummelsburg to the Münzstrasse is any further under Hitler than it was under that racketeering Republic. Come on, you can do better than that.

THE COOK: It's only play acting, Franz, we all know what you say won't be your real opinions.

THE MAIDSERVANT: Don't you see you're just acting a grumbler? Theo won't take it amiss, you can depend on it. He just wants to show us something.

THE WORKER: Right. In that case I'll say. The SA looks very fine, but I think it's shit. Give me the Maxists and the Jews.

THE COOK: Franz! Really!

THE MAIDSERVANT: How can you say that, Mr Lincke?

THE SA MAN *laughing*: For Christ sake! I'd just turn you over to the nearest cop. Not got much imagination, have you? Look, you've got to say something you might be able to wriggle out of. Sort of thing you'd hear in real life.

THE WORKER: All right, then you'll have to give me a hand and provoke me.

THE SA MAN: That went out years ago. Suppose I said 'Our Führer's the greatest man there's ever been, greater than Jesus Christ and Napoleon rolled into one,' all you'd say was 'You bet he is.' So I'd best take the other road and say: 'They're a big-mouthed lot. You know the one about Goebbels and the two fleas? Well, the two fleas had a bet who could get from one side of his mouth to the other quickest. The winner was the one went round the back of his head. It wasn't so far that way.

THE CHAUFFEUR: Ha.

All laugh.

THE SA MAN *to the worker:* Now it's your turn to make a crack.

THE WORKER: I can't cap a story like that bang off. Telling the joke wouldn't stop you being an informer.

THE MAIDSERVANT: He's right, Theo.

THE SA MAN: You're a right bunch of turds. Make me sick, you do. Not a bloody soul got the guts to open his mouth.

THE WORKER: Is that what you really think, or is it what you say at the public welfare?

THE SA MAN: I say it at the public welfare too.

THE WORKER: In that case what I say at the public welfare is Look before you leap. I'm a coward. I don't carry a gun.

THE SA MAN: Right, brother, if you're going to be so careful about looking, let me tell you you can look and look, then all of a sudden you're in the voluntary labour service.

THE WORKER: And if you don't look?

THE SA MAN: Then you'll be in it just the same. Sure. It's voluntary, see? Voluntary's good, don't you think?

THE WORKER: That's where it might be possible for some daring fellow to make a joke or two about the Voluntary Labour Service, suppose both of you were standing at the Public Welfare and you gave him one of those looks with your blue eyes. I wonder what he could say. Maybe: another fifteen went off yesterday. Funny how they get them to do it, when you think it's all voluntary and folk are paid no more for doing something than for doing nothing though they must need to eat more. Then I heard the one about Dr Ley and the cat and of course I saw the whole thing. You know that story?

THE SA MAN: No, we don't.

THE WORKER: Well, Dr Ley went on this little Strength Through Joy trip, strictly on business, and he met one of those former Weimar party bosses – I'm not up in all their names, anyway it might have been in a concentration camp though Dr Ley's got much too much sense to visit one of those – and the old boss asked him how'd he get the workers to swallow all the things they usedn't to put up with at any price. Dr Ley pointed to a cat lying in the sun and said: suppose you wanted to give that cat a mouthful of mustard and make her swallow it whether she wanted or not. How would you do it? Boss takes the mustard and smears it over the cat's chops; of course it spits it back in his face, no question of swallowing, just a lot of bloody scratches. No, old boy, says Dr Ley in his endearing way, you got the wrong approach. Now watch me. He takes the mustard with a practised follow-through and sticks it abracadabra up the wretched beast's arsehole. *To the ladies*: Excuse my French, but that's part of the story. – Numbed and stunned by the frightful pain, cat instantly sets to licking out the lot. There you are, my dear fellow, says the triumphant Dr Ley, she's eating it. And voluntarily at that! *They laugh.*

THE WORKER: Yes, it's very funny.

THE SA MAN: That's got things going. Voluntary Labour Service, that's a favourite subject. Trouble is: nobody bothers to dig his toes in. Oh, they can make us eat shit and we'll still say thank you for it.

THE WORKER: I'm not so sure about that. There am I the other day on the Alexanderplatz wondering whether to volunteer for the Voluntary Labour Service spontaneous-like or wait till they shove me in. Over from the grocer's on the corner comes a skinny little woman, must be some proletarian's wife. Half a mo, says I, what are the proletarians doing in the Third Reich when we've got national unity and even Baron Thyssen is in it? No, says she, not when they've gone and put up the price of marge. From fifty pfennigs to one mark. You trying to tell me that's national unity? Better mind out, ma, says I, what you're saying to me, I'm patriotic to the backbone. All bones and no meat, says she, and chaff in the bread. She was that worked up. I just stand there mumbling: best get butter then. It's better for you. Mustn't skimp on your food, cause that saps the people's strength and we can't afford that what with so many enemies encircling us even in the top civil service ... we been warned. No, says she, we're all of us Nazis so long as we got breath in our bodies, what mayn't be long now in view of the war menace. Only the other day I got to offer my best sofa to the Winter Aid, says she, cause I hear Goering's having to sleep on the floor he's that worried about our raw materials, and in the office they say they'd rather have a piano – you know, for Strength Through Joy. And no proper flour to be had. I takes my sofa away from the Winter Aid People and goes to the second-hand dealer round the corner, I been meaning to buy half a pound of butter for some time. And at the dairy they tell me: no butter today, comrade, would you like some guns? I say, give me, says she. I say: come on what d'you want guns for, ma? On an empty stomach? No, says she, if I'm going to be hungry they should be shot, the whole lot of them starting with Hitler at the top ... Come on, says I, come on, exclaims I appalled ... With Hitler at the top we'll conquer France, says she. Now we're getting our petrol from wool. And the wool? says I. The wool, says she: these days that's made from petrol. Wool's another thing we need. Any time a bit of good stuff from the old days reaches the Winter Aid the lot that run the place grab it for themselves, says she. If Hitler only knew, says they, but he knows nothing the poor lamb, never went to secondary school they say. I was struck dumb by so much subversiveness. You just stay here, young lady, says I, I got to make a call at police headquarters. But when I come back with an officer what d'you you think, she's cleared off. *Stops play-acting.* What d'you say to that, eh?

THE SA MAN *still acting*: Me? What do I say? Well, I might

give a reproachful look. You went straight round to the
police, I might say. Can't risk talking freely when you're
around.

THE WORKER: I should think not. Not with me. You confide
in me, you'll be done. I know my duty as a comrade: any
time my own mother mutters something to me about the
price of margarine or something I go straight to the local
SA office. I'll denounce my own brother for grumbling
about the Voluntary Labour Service. As for my girl, when
she tells me 'Heil Hitler' she's got pregnant at a work camp
then I have them bring her in: we can't have abortions
because if we made exceptions for our nearest and dearest
the Third Reich would run out of manpower, and the Third
Reich's what we love best. – Was that more like it? Did I
act all right?

THE SA MAN: I guess that'll do. *Goes on acting.* You'll be
okay, go and draw your benefit, we've all understood, eh
brothers? But you can count on me, my friend, 'nuff said,
mum's the word. *He slaps him on the shoulder. No longer
acting*: Right, then in you go into the office and they'll pick
you up bang off.

THE WORKER: What, without you leaving the line and
following me in?

THE SA MAN: Yeh.

THE WORKER: And without you giving someone a wink,
which might look fishy?

THE SA MAN: Without me winking.

THE WORKER: How's it done then?

THE SA MAN: Ha, you'd like to know that trick. Well, stand
up, and show us your back. *He turns him round by the
shoulders, so that everyone can see his back. Then to the
maidservant*: Seen it?

THE MAIDSERVANT: Look, he's got a white cross on it.

THE COOK: Right between his shoulders.

THE CHAUFFEUR: So he has.

THE SA MAN: And how did he get it? *Shows the palm of his
hand.* See, just a little white chalk cross and there's its
impression large as life.

The worker takes off his jacket and looks at the cross.

THE WORKER: Nice work.

THE SA MAN: Not bad, eh? I always have my chalk on me. Ah, you have to use your loaf, things don't always go according to the book. *With satisfaction*: Well, so it's off to Reinickendorf. *Corrects himself*: That's where my aunt lives, you know. You lot don't seem very enthusiastic. *To the maidservant*: What are you gawping like that for, Anna? Missed the whole point of the trick, I suppose?

THE MAIDSERVANT: Of course not. Think I'm silly or something?

THE SA MAN *as if the whole joke has gone sour, stretches his hand out to her*: Wipe it off.

She washes his hand with a rag.

THE COOK: You've got to use those sort of methods so long as they keep on trying to undermine everything our Führer has built up and what makes other people so envious of us.

THE CHAUFFEUR: What was that? Oh yes, quite so. *Looks at his watch*. Well, time to wash the car again. Heil Hitler! *Exit*.

THE SA MAN: What kind of a fellow's that?

THE MAIDSERVANT: Keeps himself to himself. Not a bit political.

THE WORKER: Well, Minna, I'd better be off. No hard feelings about the beer, eh? And let me say I'm surer than ever that no one's going to complain about the Third Reich and get away with it. That's set my mind at rest. Me, I don't ever come across that sort of subversive element. I'd gladly confront them if I did. Only I'm not quite so quick to the punch as you. *Clearly and distinctly*: All right, Minna, thanks a lot and Heil Hitler!

THE OTHERS: Heil Hitler!

THE SA MAN: Take a tip from me and don't be quite so innocent. It attracts attention. No call to have to watch your mouth with me, I can take a joke now and again. All right: Heil Hitler!

The worker goes.

THE SA MAN: Bit sudden the way those two cleared out. Something's put ants in their pants. I shouldn't have said that about Reinickendorf. They're waiting to pounce on that sort of thing.

THE MAIDSERVANT: There's something else I wanted to ask you, Theo.

THE SA MAN: Fire away, any time.

THE COOK: I'm off to put out the laundry. I was young once too. *Exit.*

THE SA MAN: What is it?

THE MAIDSERVANT: But I shan't ask unless I can see you won't mind; otherwise I'll say nothing.

THE SA MAN: Spit it out, then.

THE MAIDSERVANT: It's just that ... I don't like saying ... well, I need 20 marks from your account.

THE SA MAN: Twenty marks?

THE MAIDSERVANT: There you are, you *do* mind.

THE SA MAN: Twenty marks out of our savings account, can't expect me to give three cheers. What do you want it for?

THE MAIDSERVANT: I'd rather not say.

THE SA MAN: So. You're not saying. That's a laugh.

THE MAIDSERVANT: I know you won't agree with me, Theo, so I'd sooner not give my reasons yet awhile.

THE SA MAN: Well, if you don't trust me ...

THE MAIDSERVANT: Of course I trust you.

THE SA MAN: So you want to give up having a joint savings account?

THE MAIDSERVANT: How can you say that? If I take out twenty marks I'll still have ninety-seven marks left.

THE SA MAN: No need to do sums for my benefit. I know how much there is. I just think you're wanting to break it off, probably because you're flirting with someone else. Perhaps you'll be wanting to check our statement too.

THE MAIDSERVANT: I'm not flirting with anyone else.

THE SA MAN: Then tell me what it's for.

THE MAIDSERVANT: You don't want to let me have it.

THE SA MAN: How am I to tell it isn't for something wrong?

THE MAIDSERVANT: It's not anything wrong, and if I didn't need it I wouldn't call for it, you must know that.

THE SA MAN: I don't know nothing. All I know is the whole business strikes me as rather fishy. Why should you suddenly need twenty marks? It's quite a bit of money. You pregnant?

THE MAIDSERVANT: No.

THE SA MAN: Sure?

THE MAIDSERVANT: Yes.

THE SA MAN: If I thought for a minute you were planning anything illegal, if I caught a whiff of that kind of thing, I'd be down like a ton of bricks, let me tell you. You might just have heard that any interference with our burgeoning fruit is the worst crime you can commit. If the German people stopped multiplying itself it would be all up with our historic mission.

THE MAIDSERVANT: But Theo, I don't know what you're talking about. It's nothing like that, I'd have told you if it was because you'd be involved too. But if that's what you're thinking then let me tell you. It's just I want to help Frieda buy a winter coat.

THE SA MAN: And why can't your sister buy her coats for herself?

THE MAIDSERVANT: How could she on her disability pension, it's twenty-six marks eighty a month.

THE SA MAN: What about our Winter Aid? But that's just it, you've no confidence in our National Socialist state. I can tell that anyway from the sort of conversations that go on in this kitchen. Do you think I didn't see what a long face you pulled at my experiment?

THE MAIDSERVANT: What do you mean by a long face?

THE SA MAN: You pulled one all right. Just like our friends who cleared out so suddenly.

THE MAIDSERVANT: If you really want to know what I think, I don't like that kind of thing.

THE SA MAN: And what is it you don't like, may I ask?

THE MAIDSERVANT: The way you catch those poor down-and-outs by dressing up and playing tricks and all that. My father's unemployed too.

THE SA MAN: Ha, that's all I needed to hear. As if talking to that fellow Lincke hadn't already set me thinking.

THE MAIDSERVANT: Do you mean to say you're going to nail

him for what he did just to please you and with all of us egging him on?

THE SA MAN: I'm not saying nothing. As I already told you. And if you've anything against what I'm doing as part of my duty then let me say just look in *Mein Kampf* and you'll see how the Führer himself didn't think it beneath him to test the people's attitude of mind, and it was actually his job for a while when he was in the army and it was all for Germany and the consequences were tremendously important.

THE MAIDSERVANT: If that's your line, Theo, then I'd just like to know if I can have the twenty marks. That's all.

THE SA MAN: Then all I can say to you is I'm not in the mood to have anything taken off me.

THE MAIDSERVANT: What do you mean, taken off you? Whose money is it, yours or mine?

THE SA MAN: That's a nice way to be speaking about our joint money all of a sudden. I suppose that's why we purged the Jews from the life of our nation, so we could have our own kith and kin suck our blood instead?

THE MAIDSERVANT: How can you say things like that on account of twenty marks?

THE SA MAN: I've plenty of expenses. My boots alone set me back twenty-seven marks.

THE MAIDSERVANT: But weren't they issued to you?

THE SA MAN: That's what we thought. And that's why I took the better kind, the ones with gaiters. Then they demanded payment and we were stung.

THE MAIDSERVANT: Twenty-seven marks for boots? So what other expenses were there?

THE SA MAN: What d'you mean, other expenses?

THE MAIDSERVANT: Didn't you say you had lots of expenses?

THE SA MAN: Forgotten what they were. Anyway I'm not here to be cross-examined. Keep your hair on, I'm not going to swindle you. And as for the twenty marks I'll think it over.

THE MAIDSERVANT *weeping*: Theo, I just can't believe you'd tell me the money was all right and it wasn't true. Oh now I don't know what to think. Surely there's twenty marks left in the savings bank out of all that money?

THE SA MAN *slapping her on the shoulder*: But nobody's suggesting for a minute that there's nothing left in our savings bank. Out of the question. You know you can rely on me. You trust something to me, it's like locking it in the safe. Well, decided to trust Theo again, have you?
She weeps without replying.

THE SA MAN: It's just nerves, you've been working too hard. Well, time I went off to that night exercise. I'll be coming for you on Friday, then. Heil Hitler! *Exit.*
The maidservant tries to suppress her tears and walks distractedly up and down the kitchen. The cook comes back with a basket of linen.

THE COOK: What's wrong? Had a quarrel? Theo's such a splendid boy. Pity there aren't more like him. Nothing serious, is it?

THE MAIDSERVANT *still weeping*: Minna, can't you go out to your brother's and tell him to watch out for himself?

THE COOK: What for?

THE MAIDSERVANT: Just watch out, I mean.

THE COOK: On account of tonight? You can't be serious. Theo would never do such a thing.

THE MAIDSERVANT: I don't know what to think any longer, Minna. He's changed so. They've completely ruined him. He's keeping bad company. Four years we've been going out together, and now it seems to me just as though ... I even feel like asking you to look at my shoulder and see if there's a white cross on it.

4

Peat-bog soldiers

> With storm troopers parading
> These men carry on debating
> What Lenin and Kautsky meant
> Till, clutching the tomes they've cited

They're forcibly united
By joint imprisonment.

Esterwegen concentration camp, 1934. Some prisoners are mixing cement.

BRÜHL *softly to Dievenbach*: I'd steer clear of Lohmann; he talks.

DIEVENBACH *aloud*: Oi, Lohmann, here's Brühl saying I should steer clear of you; you talk.

BRÜHL: Bastard.

LOHMANN: That's good coming from you, you bloody Judas. Why did Karl get given solitary?

BRÜHL: Nothing to do with me. Was it me got cigarettes from God knows where?

THE JEHOVAH'S WITNESS: Look out.

The SS sentry up on the embankment goes by.

THE SS MAN: Someone was talking here. Who was it? *Nobody answers.* If that happens just once more it'll be solitary confinement for the lot of you, get me? Now sing! *The prisoners sing verse 1 of the 'Song of the Peat-bog Soldiers'. The SS man moves on.*

PRISONERS:
See, whichever way one gazes
Naught but boggy heath lies there.
Not one bird his sweet voice raises
In those oak trees gaunt and bare.
    We are the peat-bog soldiers
    With shovels on our shoulders
    We march.

THE JEHOVAH'S WITNESS: Why do you people carry on quarrelling even now?

DIEVENBACH: Don't you worry, Jehovah, you wouldn't understand. *Indicating Brühl*: Yesterday his party voted for Hitler's foreign policy in the Reichstag. And he – *indicating Lohmann* – thinks Hitler's foreign policy means war.

BRÜHL: Not with us around.

LOHMANN: Last war we had you were around all right.

BRÜHL: Anyway the German armed forces are too weak.

LOHMANN: Still, your lot did at least bring Hitler a battle-cruiser as part of the wedding deal.

THE JEHOVAH'S WITNESS *to Dievenbach*: What were you? Communist or Social-democrat?

DIEVENBACH: I kept outside all that.

LOHMANN: But you're inside now all right, inside a camp I mean.

THE JEHOVAH'S WITNESS: Look out.

The SS man appears again. He watches them. Slowly Brühl starts singing the third verse of the 'Song of the Peat-bog Soldiers'. The SS man moves on.

BRÜHL:
Back and forth the guards keep pacing
Not a soul can get away.
Shots for those who try escaping
Thick barbed wire for those who stay.
    We are the peat-bog soldiers
    With shovels on our shoulders
    We march.

LOHMANN *hurls his shovel from him*: When I think I'm only in here because your lot sabotaged the united front I could bash your bloody brains out right now.

BRÜHL: Ha! 'Like your brother must I be/Or you'll turn and clobber me' – is that it? United front indeed. Softly softly catchee monkey: would have suited you nicely to sneak all our members away, wouldn't it?

LOHMANN: When you'd rather have Hitler sneak them away, like now. You traitors!

BRÜHL *furiously takes his shovel and brandishes it at Lohmann, who holds his own shovel at the ready*: I'll teach you something you won't forget!

THE JEHOVAH'S WITNESS: Look out.

He hastily starts singing the last verse of the 'Song of the Peat-bog Soldiers'. The SS man reappears and the others join in as they resume mixing their cement.

We've no use for caterwauling.
Sunshine follows after rain.
One day soon you'll hear us calling:

Homeland, you are ours again.
  And then we peat-bog soldiers
  Will rise, throw back our shoulders
  And march.

THE SS MAN: Which of you shouted 'Traitors'?
Nobody answers.
THE SS MAN: You people never learn, do you? *To Lohmann:*
Which?
Lohmann stares at Brühl and says nothing.
THE SS MAN *to Dievenbach*: Which?
Dievenbach says nothing.
THE SS MAN *to the Jehovah's Witness*: Which?
The Jehovah's Witness says nothing.
THE SS MAN *to Brühl*: Which?
Brühl says nothing.
THE SS MAN: I shall count up to five, then it'll be solitary
confinement for the whole lot of you till you turn blue.
*He waits for five seconds. They all stand in silence staring
straight ahead.*
THE SS MAN: So it's solitary.

5
Servants of the people

  The camps are run by warders
  Narks, butchers and marauders –
  The people's servants they
  They'll crush you and assail you
  And flog you and impale you
  For negligible pay.

*Oranienburg concentration camp, 1934. A small yard
between the huts. In the darkness a sound of flogging. As it
gets light an SS man is seen flogging a detainee. An SS officer
stands in the background smoking; with his back to the scene.
Then he goes off.*

THE SS MAN *sits down on a barrel, exhausted*: Work on.

The detainee rises from the ground and starts unsteadily cleaning the drains.

Why can't you say no when they ask if you're a communist, you cunt? It means the lash for you and I have to stay in barracks. I'm so fucking tired. Why can't they give the job to Klapproth? He enjoys this sort of thing. Look, if that bastard comes round again – *he listens* – you're to take the whip and flog the ground hard as you can, right?

THE DETAINEE: Yes, sir.

THE SS MAN: But only because you buggers have flogged me out, right?

THE DETAINEE: Yes, sir.

THE SS MAN: Here he comes.

Steps are heard outside, and the SS man points to the whip. The detainee picks it up and flogs the ground. This doesn't sound authentic, so the SS man idly points to a nearby basket which the detainee then flogs. The steps outside come to a stop. The SS man abruptly rises in some agitation, snatches the whip and begins beating the detainee.

THE DETAINEE *softly*: Not my stomach.

The SS man hits him on the bottom. The SS officer looks in.

THE SS OFFICER: Flog his stomach.

The SS man beats the detainee's stomach.

6

Judicial process

> The judges follow limply.
> They were told that justice is simply
> What serves our People best.
> They objected: how are we to know that?
> But they'll soon be interpreting it so that
> The whole people is under arrest.

Augsburg 1934. Consultation room in a court building. A milky January morning can be seen through the window. A spherical gas lamp is still burning. The district judge is just putting on his robes. There is a knock.

THE JUDGE: Come in.
Enter the police inspector.
THE INSPECTOR: Good morning, your honour.
THE JUDGE: Good morning, Mr Tallinger. It's about the case of Häberle, Schünt and Gaunitzer. I must admit the whole affair is a bit beyond me.
THE INSPECTOR: ?
THE JUDGE: I understand from the file that the shop where the incident occurred – Arndt's the jeweller's – is a Jewish one?
THE INSPECTOR: ?
THE JUDGE: And presumably Häberle, Schünt and Gaunitzer are still members of Storm Troop 7?
The inspector nods.
THE JUDGE: Which means that the Troop saw no reason to discipline them?
The inspector shakes his head.
THE JUDGE: All the same, I take it the Troop must have instituted some kind of inquiry in view of the disturbance which the incident caused in the neighbourhood?
The inspector shrugs his shoulders.
THE JUDGE: I would appreciate it, Tallinger, if you would give me a brief summary before we go into court. Would you?
THE INSPECTOR *mechanically*: On 2 December 1933 at 0815 hours SA men Häberle, Schünt and Gaunitzer forced their way into Arndt's jewellers in the Schlettowstrasse and after a brief exchange of words wounded Mr Arndt age 54 on the head. The material damage amounted to a total of eleven thousand two hundred and thirty-four marks. Inquiries were instituted by the criminal investigation department on 7 December 1933 and led to . . .
THE JUDGE: Come on, Tallinger, that's all in the files. *He points irritably at the charge sheet, which consists of a single page.* This is the flimsiest and sloppiest made-out indictment I've ever seen, not that the last few months have been much of a picnic, let me tell you. But it does say that much.

I was hoping you might be able to tell me a bit about the background.

THE INSPECTOR: Yes, your honour.

THE JUDGE: Well, then?

THE INSPECTOR: There isn't any background to this case, your honour, so to speak.

THE JUDGE: Tallinger, are you trying to tell me it's all clear as daylight?

THE INSPECTOR *grinning*: Clear as daylight: no.

THE JUDGE: Various items of jewellery are alleged to have vanished in the course of the incident. Have they been recovered?

THE INSPECTOR: Not to my knowledge: no.

THE JUDGE: ?

THE INSPECTOR: Your honour, I've got a family.

THE JUDGE: So have I, Tallinger.

THE INSPECTOR: Yes, sir.

Pause.

THE INSPECTOR: This Arndt fellow is a Jew, you know.

THE JUDGE: So one would infer from the name.

THE INSPECTOR: Yes, sir. There's been a rumour for some time in the neighbourhood that there was a case of racial profanation.

THE JUDGE *begins to get a glimmer*: Indeed. Involving whom?

THE INSPECTOR: Arndt's daughter. She's nineteen and supposed to be pretty.

THE JUDGE: Was there any official follow-up?

THE INSPECTOR *reluctantly*: Well, no. The rumour died a natural death.

THE JUDGE: Who set it going?

THE INSPECTOR: The landlord of the building. A certain Mr von Miehl.

THE JUDGE: I suppose he wanted the Jewish shop out of his building?

THE INSPECTOR: That's what we thought. But then he seems to have changed his line.

THE JUDGE: At least that would explain why there was a certain amount of resentment against Arndt round there.

Leading these young people to act from a kind of upsurge
of national feeling ...

THE INSPECTOR *firmly*: I wouldn't say that, your honour.

THE JUDGE: What wouldn't you say?

THE INSPECTOR: That Häberle, Schünt and Gaunitzer will
try to get much mileage out of the racial profanation
business.

THE JUDGE: Why not?

THE INSPECTOR: As I told you, there hasn't been any official
mention of the name of the Aryan involved. It could be
anyone. Anywhere there's a bunch of Aryans you might
find him, you get me? And where d'you find those bunches
of Aryans? In other words the SA don't want this dragged
up.

THE JUDGE *impatiently*: Why tell me about it, then?

THE INSPECTOR: Because you said you'd got a family. To
stop you dragging it up. Any of the local witnesses might
mention it.

THE JUDGE: I see. But I can't see much else.

THE INSPECTOR: The less the better, if you want my personal
opinion.

THE JUDGE: It's easy for you to say that. I have to deliver a
judgement.

THE INSPECTOR *vaguely*: That's right ...

THE JUDGE: So we're left with a direct provocation on
Arndt's part, or else there's no way of explaining what
happened.

THE INSPECTOR: Just what I'd say myself, your honour.

THE JUDGE: Then how were those SA people provoked?

THE INSPECTOR: According to their statements: partly by
Arndt himself and partly by some unemployed man he'd
got in to sweep the snow. Apparently they were on their
way to have a beer together and as they passed the shop
there were Wagner the unemployed man and Arndt himself
standing in the doorway and shouting vulgar terms of abuse
at them.

THE JUDGE: I don't suppose they have any witnesses, have
they?

THE INSPECTOR: Oh, they have. The landlord – you know,

von Miehl – said he was at the window and saw Wagner provoking the SA men. And Arndt's partner, a man called Stau, was round at Troop HQ the same afternoon and admitted in front of Häberle, Schünt and Gaunitzer that Arndt had always talked disparagingly about the SA, to him too.

THE JUDGE: Oh, so Arndt's got a partner? Aryan?

THE INSPECTOR: Aryan: what else? Can you really see him taking on a Jew as his front man?

THE JUDGE: But the partner wouldn't go and give evidence against him?

THE INSPECTOR *slyly*: Who's to say?

THE JUDGE *irritated*: What do you mean? There's no way the firm can claim damages if it can be proved that Arndt provoked Häberle, Schünt and Gaunitzer to assault him.

THE INSPECTOR: What makes you think Stau's interested in claiming damages?

THE JUDGE: I don't get you. Surely he's a partner?

THE INSPECTOR: That's it.

THE JUDGE: ?

THE INSPECTOR: We've found out – unofficially of course and off the record – that Stau's a regular visitor to Troop HQ. He used to be in the SA and may still be. Probably that's what made Arndt make him a partner. What's more, Stau's already been mixed up in a similar affair, where the SA dropped in on someone. They picked the wrong man that time and it took quite a bit of effort to get it all swept under the mat. Of course that's not to say that in our particular case Stau ... Well, anyhow he's someone to be careful of. I hope you'll treat this as completely confidential, given what you said about your family earlier.

THE JUDGE *shaking his head*: I don't quite see how it can be in Mr Stau's interest for his business to lose more than eleven thousand marks.

THE INSPECTOR: Yes, the jewellery has disappeared. Anyhow Häberle, Schünt and Gaunitzer haven't got it. And they haven't fenced it either.

THE JUDGE: Indeed.

THE INSPECTOR: Stau naturally can't be expected to keep

Arndt on as his partner if Arndt can be shown to have acted
in a provocative way. And any loss he has caused will have
to be made up to Stau, see?

THE JUDGE: Yes, I do indeed see. *For a moment he looks
thoughtfully at the inspector, who resumes his blank official
expression.* Yes, then I suppose the long and the short of it
will be that Arndt provoked the SA men. It seems that the
fellow had made himself generally disliked. Didn't you tell
me that the goings-on in his own family had already led the
landlord to complain? Ah well, I know this shouldn't really
be dragged up, but anyway we can take it that there will be
relief in those quarters if he moves out shortly. Thank you
very much, Tallinger, you've been a great help.

*The judge gives the inspector a cigar. The inspector leaves.
In the doorway he meets the official prosecutor, who is just
entering.*

THE PROSECUTOR *to the judge*: Can I have a word with you?

THE JUDGE *as he peels an apple for his breakfast*: You can
indeed.

THE PROSECUTOR: It's about the case of Häberle, Schünt and
Gaunitzer.

THE JUDGE *otherwise occupied*: Yes?

THE PROSECUTOR: It seems quite a straightforward case on
the face of it . . .

THE JUDGE: Right. I really don't see why your department
decided to prosecute, if you don't mind my saying so.

THE PROSECUTOR: What do you mean? The case has caused a
deplorable stir in the neighbourhood. Even members of the
party have thought it ought to be cleared up.

THE JUDGE: I simply see it as a plain case of Jewish
provocation, that's all.

THE PROSECUTOR: Oh, rubbish, Goll! Don't imagine our
indictments can be dismissed so lightly just because they
seem a bit tersely expressed these days. I could have guessed
you'd blithely settle for the most obvious interpretation.
Better not make a boob of this. It doesn't take long to get
transferred to the Silesian backwoods. And it's not all that
cosy there these days.

THE JUDGE *puzzled, stops eating his apple*: I don't understand that one little bit. Are you seriously telling me you propose to let the Jew Arndt go free?

THE PROSECUTOR *expansively*: You bet I am. The fellow had no idea of provoking anyone. Are you suggesting that because he's Jewish he can't expect justice in the courts of the Third Reich? That's some pretty queer opinions you're venting there, Goll.

THE JUDGE *irritably*: I was venting no opinions whatever. I simply concluded that Häberle, Schünt and Gaunitzer were provoked.

THE PROSECUTOR: But can't you see it wasn't Arndt who provoked them but that unemployed fellow, what's his damn name, the one clearing the snow, yes, Wagner?

THE JUDGE: There's not one single word about that in your indictment, my dear Spitz.

THE PROSECUTOR: Of course not. It merely came to the attention of the Prosecutor's office that those SA men had made an assault on Arndt. Which meant that we were officially bound to take action. But if witness von Miehl should testify in court that Arndt wasn't in the street at all during the dispute, whereas that unemployed fellow, what's his damn name, yes, Wagner, was hurling insults at the SA, then it will have to be taken into account.

THE JUDGE *tumbling to earth*: Is that what von Miehl is supposed to be saying? But he's the landlord who wants to get Arndt out of his building. He's not going to give evidence for him.

THE PROSECUTOR: Come on, what have you got against von Miehl? Why shouldn't he tell the truth under oath? Perhaps you don't realise that, quite apart from the fact that he's in the SS, von Miehl has pretty good contacts in the Ministry of Justice? My advice to you, Goll old man, is to treat him as a man of honour.

THE JUDGE: That's what I'm doing. After all, you can't call it exactly dishonourable these days not to want a Jewish shop in one's building.

THE PROSECUTOR *generously*: If the fellow pays his rent...

THE JUDGE *diplomatically*: I believe he's supposed to have reported him already on another matter...

THE PROSECUTOR: So you're aware of that? But who told you it was in order to get the fellow out? Particularly as the complaint was withdrawn? That suggests something more like a particularly close understanding, wouldn't you say? My dear Goll, how can you be so naive?

THE JUDGE *now getting really annoyed*: My dear Spitz, it's not that simple. The partner I thought would want to cover him wants to report him, and the landlord who reported him wants to cover him. You have to know the ins and outs.

THE PROSECUTOR: What do we draw our pay for?

THE JUDGE: Shockingly mixed-up business. Have a Havana? *The prosecutor takes a Havana and they smoke in silence. Then the judge gloomily reflects.*

THE JUDGE: But suppose it's established in court that Arndt never provoked anybody, then he can go on and sue the SA for damages.

THE PROSECUTOR: To start with he can't sue the SA but only Häberle, Schünt and Gaunitzer, who haven't a penny – that's if he doesn't simply have to make do with that unemployed fellow, what's his damn name ... got it, Wagner. *With emphasis*: Secondly he may think twice before suing members of the SA.

THE JUDGE: Where is he at the moment?

THE PROSECUTOR: In hospital.

THE JUDGE: And Wagner?

THE PROSECUTOR: In a concentration camp.

THE JUDGE *with a certain relief*: Oh well, in those circumstances I don't suppose Arndt will be wanting to sue the SA. And Wagner won't be particularly keen to make a big thing of his innocence. But the SA aren't going to be all that pleased if the Jew gets off scot free.

THE PROSECUTOR: The SA will have proof in court that they were provoked. By the Jew or by the Marxist, it's all the same to them.

THE JUDGE *still dubious*: Not entirely. After all the dispute between the SA and the unemployed man did result in damage to the shop. Storm Troop 7 isn't altogether in the clear.

THE PROSECUTOR: Oh well, you can't have everything. You'll never be able to satisfy all parties. As for which you should aim to satisfy, that's a matter for your sense of patriotism, my dear Goll. All I can say is that patriotic circles – by which I mean the highest quarters of the SS – are looking to the German judiciary to show a bit more backbone.

THE JUDGE *with a deep sigh*: The process of law is getting a bit complicated these days, my dear Spitz, you must admit.

THE PROSECUTOR: Of course. But you have an excellent remark by our Minister of Justice to guide you. Justice is what serves the German people best.

THE JUDGE *apathetically*: Mm yes.

THE PROSECUTOR: Mustn't let it get you down, that's all. *He gets up.* So now you've got the background. Should be plain sailing. See you later, my dear Goll.

He leaves. The judge is not at all happy. He stands by the window for a while. Then he leafs aimlessly through his papers. Finally he presses the bell. A court usher enters.

THE JUDGE: Go and find Detective-Inspector Tallinger in the witnesses' room and bring him back here. Discreetly.

Exit the usher. Then the inspector reappears.

THE JUDGE: Tallinger, you nearly landed me in the cart with your idea of treating this as a case of provocation on Arndt's part. Apparently Mr von Miehl is all set to swear that it was Wagner the unemployed man who did the provoking and not Arndt.

THE INSPECTOR *giving nothing away*: So they say, your honour.

THE JUDGE: What's that mean: 'so they say'?

THE INSPECTOR: That Wagner shouted the offensive remarks.

THE JUDGE: Isn't it true?

THE INSPECTOR *offended*: Your honour, whether it's true or not it's not something we can . . .

THE JUDGE *firmly*: Listen to me, Detective-Inspector Tallinger. This is a German court you're in. Has Wagner admitted that or has he not?

THE INSPECTOR: Your honour, I didn't go to the concentration camp myself, if you want to know. The official report

of his deposition – Wagner's supposed to have got something wrong with his kidneys – says that he admitted it. It's
only that . . .

THE JUDGE: There you are, he did admit it. It's only that
what?

THE INSPECTOR: He served in the war and was wounded in
the neck, and according to Stau, you know, Arndt's partner,
he can't talk above a whisper. So how von Miehl could have
heard him from the first floor hurling insults isn't
entirely . . .

THE JUDGE: I imagine it will be said that you don't need a
voice in order to tell someone to 'get stuffed', as they put it.
You can do it with a simple gesture. It's my impression the
Prosecutor's department want to provide the SA with some
way out of that sort. More precisely, of that sort and no
other.

THE INSPECTOR: Yes, your honour.

THE JUDGE: What is Arndt's statement?

THE INSPECTOR: That he had no part in it and just hurt his
head falling down the stairs. That's all we can get out of
him.

THE JUDGE: The fellow's probably quite innocent and got
into it accidentally, like Pontius Pilate and the Creed.

THE INSPECTOR *gives up*: Yes, your honour.

THE JUDGE: And it should be good enough for the SA if their
men get off.

THE INSPECTOR: Yes, your honour.

THE JUDGE: Don't stand there saying 'yes, your honour' like
a damn metronome.

THE INSPECTOR: Yes, your honour.

THE JUDGE: What are you trying to tell me? Don't get on
your high horse now, Tallinger. You must make allowances
for my being a bit on edge. I realise you're an honest man.
And when you advised me you must have had something at
the back of your mind?

THE INSPECTOR *being a kindly soul, plunges in*: Hasn't it
struck you that our deputy prosecutor might simply be
after your job and is putting the skids under you, sir?
That's what they're saying. – Look at it this way, your

honour: you find the Jew not guilty. He never provoked a soul. Wasn't around. Got his head bashed in by pure accident, some quarrel between a different lot of people. Then after a while, back he comes to the shop. No way Stau can prevent it. And the shop is about eleven thousand marks short. Stau will be just as hit by this loss, because now he can't claim the eleven thousand back from Arndt. So Stau, from what I know of his sort, is going to tackle the SA about his jewels. He can't approach them in person because being in partnership with a Jew counts as being sold out to Judah. But he'll have people who can. Then it will come out that the SA go pinching jewels in an upsurge of national feeling. You can guess for yourself how Storm Troop 7 is going to look at your verdict. And the man in the street won't understand anyway. Because how can it be possible for a Jew to win a case against the SA under the Third Reich?

For some while there has been noise off. It now becomes quite loud.

THE JUDGE: What's that shocking noise? Just a minute, Tallinger. *He rings. The usher comes in.* What's that din, man?

THE USHER: The courtroom's full. And now they're jammed so tight in the corridors that nobody can get through. And there are some people from the SA there who say they've got to get through because they've orders to attend.

Exit the usher, while the judge just looks scared.

THE INSPECTOR *continuing*: Those people are going to be a bit of a nuisance to you, you know. I'd advise you to concentrate on Arndt and not stir up the SA.

THE JUDGE *sits brokenly, holding his head in his hands. In a weary voice*: All right, Tallinger, I'll have to think it over.

THE INSPECTOR: That's the idea, your honour.

He leaves. The judge gets up with difficulty and rings insistently. Enter the usher.

THE JUDGE: Just go over and ask Judge Fey of the High Court if he'd mind looking in for a moment.

The usher goes. Enter the judge's maidservant with his packed breakfast.

THE MAIDSERVANT: You'll be forgetting your own head next, your honour. You're a terrible man. What did you forget this time? Try and think. The most important thing of all! *She hands him the packet.* Your breakfast! You'll be going off again and buying those rolls hot from the oven and next thing we'll have another stomach-ache like last week. Because you don't look after yourself properly.

THE JUDGE: That'll do, Marie.

THE MAIDSERVANT: Had a job getting through, I did. The whole building's full of brownshirts on account of the trial. But they'll get it hot and strong today, won't they, your honour? Like at the butcher's folk were saying 'good thing there's still some justice left'. Going and beating a business man up! Half the SA used to be criminals; it's common knowledge in the neighbourhood. If we didn't have justice they'd be making away with the cathedral. After the rings, they were; that Häberle's got a girl friend who was on the game till six months ago. And they attacked Wagner, him with the neck wound and no job, when he was shovelling snow with everyone looking on. They're quite open about it, just terrorising the neighbourhood, and if anybody says anything they lay for him and beat him senseless.

THE JUDGE: All right, Marie. Just run along now.

THE MAIDSERVANT: I told them in the butcher's: his honour will show them where they get off, right? All the decent folk are on your side, that's a fact, your honour. Only don't eat your breakfast too quickly, it might do you harm. It's so bad for the health, and now I'll be off and not hold you up, you'll have to be going into court, and don't get worked up in court or perhaps you'd better eat first, it'll only take a few minutes and they won't matter and you shouldn't eat when your stomach's all tensed up. Because you should take better care of yourself. Your health's your most precious possession, but now I'll be off, there's no need to tell you and I can see you're raring to get on with the case and I've got to go to the grocer's still.

Exit the maidservant. Enter Judge Fey of the High Court, an elderly judge with whom the district judge is friends.

THE SENIOR JUDGE: What's up?

THE JUDGE: I've got something I'd like to discuss with you if you've a moment. I'm sitting on a pretty ghastly case this morning.

THE SENIOR JUDGE *sitting down*: I know, the SA case.

THE JUDGE *stops pacing around*: How d'you know about that?

THE SENIOR JUDGE: It came up in discussion yesterday afternoon. A nasty business.

The judge starts again nervously pacing up and down.

THE JUDGE: What are they saying over your side?

THE SENIOR JUDGE: You aren't envied. *Intrigued*: What'll you do?

THE JUDGE: That's just what I'd like to know. I must say I didn't realise this case had become so famous.

THE SENIOR JUDGE *slightly amazed*: Indeed?

THE JUDGE: That partner is said to be a rather disagreeable customer.

THE SENIOR JUDGE: So I gather. Not that von Miehl is much of a humanitarian either.

THE JUDGE: Is anything known about him?

THE SENIOR JUDGE: Enough to go on with. He's got those sort of contacts.

Pause.

THE JUDGE: Very high ones?

THE SENIOR JUDGE: Very high.

Pause.

THE SENIOR JUDGE *cautiously*: Suppose you leave the Jew out of it and acquit Häberle, Schünt and Gaunitzer on the ground that the unemployed man provoked them before he dodged back into the shop, I imagine the SA might find that all right? Arndt won't sue the SA in any case.

THE JUDGE *anxiously*: There's Arndt's partner. He'll go to the SA and ask for his valuables back. And then, you know, Fey, I'll have the whole SA leadership gunning for me.

THE SENIOR JUDGE *after considering this argument, which apparently has taken him by surprise*: But suppose you don't leave the Jew out of it, then von Miehl will bring bigger guns to bear, to put it mildly. Perhaps you didn't realise he's being pressed by his bank? Arndt's his lifebelt.

THE JUDGE *appalled*: Pressed by his bank!

There is a knock.

THE SENIOR JUDGE: Come in!

Enter the usher.

THE USHER: Your honour, I really don't know what to do about keeping seats for the Chief State Prosecutor and President Schönling of the High Court. If only their honours would let one know in time.

THE SENIOR JUDGE *since the judge says nothing*: Clear two seats and don't interrupt us.

Exit the usher.

THE JUDGE: That's something I could have done without.

THE SENIOR JUDGE: Whatever happens, von Miehl can't afford to abandon Arndt and let him be ruined. He needs him.

THE JUDGE *crushed*: Someone he can milk.

THE SENIOR JUDGE: I said nothing of the sort, my dear Goll. And it seems to me quite extraordinary that you should imply I did. Let me make it crystal clear that I've not said one word against Mr von Miehl. I regret having to do so, Goll.

THE JUDGE *getting worked up*: But Fey, you can't take it that way. Not in view of our mutual relationship.

THE SENIOR JUDGE: What on earth do you mean, 'our mutual relationship'? I can't interfere in your cases. You have to choose for yourself whose toes you are going to tread on, the SA or the Ministry of Justice; either way it's your decision and nobody else's. These days everybody's his own best friend.

THE JUDGE: Of course I'm my own best friend. But what do I advise myself to do?

He stands by the door, listening to the noise outside.

THE SENIOR JUDGE: A bad business.

THE JUDGE *agitatedly*: I'll do anything, my God, can't you see my position? You've changed so. I'll give my judgement this way or that way, whatever way they want me to, but I've got to know first what they want me to do. If one doesn't know that, there's no justice left.

THE SENIOR JUDGE: I wouldn't go round shouting that there's no justice left if I were you, Goll.

THE JUDGE: Oh God, what have I said now? That's not what I meant. I just mean that with so many conflicting interests . . .

THE SENIOR JUDGE: There are no conflicting interests in the Third Reich.

THE JUDGE: Of course not. I wasn't saying there were. Don't keep weighing every single word of mine on your scales.

THE SENIOR JUDGE: Why shouldn't I? I am a judge.

THE JUDGE *who is breaking into a sweat*: But Fey, if every word uttered by every judge had to be weighed like that! I'm prepared to go over everything in the most careful and conscientious possible way, but I have to be told what kind of a decision will satisfy higher considerations. If I allow the Jew to have stayed inside the shop then I'll upset the landlord – I mean the partner; I'm getting muddled – and if the provocation came from the unemployed man then it'll be the landlord who – yes, but von Miehl would rather – Look, they can't pack me off to the backwoods in Silesia, I've got a hernia and I'm not getting embroiled with the SA, Fey, after all I've a family. It's easy for my wife to say I should just find out what actually happened. I'd wake up in hospital if nothing worse. Do I talk about assault? No, I'll talk about provocation. So what's wanted? I shan't condemn the SA of course but only the Jew or the unemployed man, only which of the two should I condemn? How do I decide between unemployed man and Jew or between partner and landlord. Whatever happens I'm not going to Silesia, Fey, I'd rather a concentration camp, the whole thing's impossible. Don't look at me like that. I'm not in the dock. I'm prepared to do absolutely anything.

THE SENIOR JUDGE *who has got to his feet*: Being prepared isn't enough, my dear fellow.

THE JUDGE: But how am I to make my decision?

THE SENIOR JUDGE: Usually a judge goes by what his conscience tells him, Judge Goll. Let that be your guide. It has been a pleasure.

THE JUDGE: Yes, of course: to the best of my heart and

conscience. But here and now; what's my choice to be, Fey? What?

The senior judge has left. The judge looks wordlessly after him. The telephone rings.

THE JUDGE *picks up the receiver*: Yes? – Emmy? – What have they put off? Our skittles session? – Who was it rang? – Priesnitz, the one who's just taken his finals? Where did he get the message? – What I'm talking about? I've got a judgement to deliver.

He hangs up. The usher enters. The noise in the corridors becomes obtrusive.

THE USHER: Häberle, Schünt, Gaunitzer, your honour.

THE JUDGE *collecting his papers*: One moment.

THE USHER: I've put the President of the High Court at the press table. He was quite happy about it. But the Chief State Prosecutor refused to take a seat among the witnesses. He wanted to be on the bench, I think. Then you'd have had to preside from the dock, your honour! *He laughs foolishly at his own joke.*

THE JUDGE: Whatever happens I'm not doing that.

THE USHER: This way out, your honour. But where's your folder got to with the indictment?

THE JUDGE *utterly confused*: Oh yes, I'll need that. Or I won't know who's being accused, will I? What the devil are we to do with the Chief State Prosecutor?

THE USHER: But your honour, that's your address book you've picked up. Here's the file.

He pushes it under the judge's arm. Wiping the sweat off his face, the judge goes distractedly out.

7

Occupational disease

> And as for the physicians
> The State gives them positions
> And pays them so much a piece.
> Their job is to keep mending

The bits the police keep sending
Then send it all back to the police.

Berlin 1934. A ward in the Charité Hospital. A new patient has been brought in. Nurses are busy writing his name on the slate at the head of his bed. Two patients in neighbouring beds are talking.

THE FIRST PATIENT: Know anything about him?

THE SECOND: I saw them bandaging him downstairs. He was on a stretcher quite close to me. He was still conscious then, but when I asked what he'd got he didn't answer. His whole body's one big wound.

THE FIRST: No need to ask then, was there?

THE SECOND: I didn't see till they started bandaging him.

ONE OF THE NURSES: Quiet please, it's the professor.

Followed by a train of assistants and nurses the surgeon enters the ward. He stops by one of the beds and pontificates.

THE SURGEON: Gentlemen, we have here a quite beautiful case showing how essential it is to ask questions and keep on searching for the deeper causes of the disease if medicine is not to degenerate into mere quackery. This patient has all the symptoms of neuralgia and for a considerable time he received the appropriate treatment. In fact however he suffers from Raynaud's Disease, which he contracted in the course of his job as a worker operating pneumatically powered tools; that is to say, gentlemen, an occupational disease. We have now begun treating him correctly. His case will show you what a mistake it is to treat the patient as a mere component of the clinic instead of asking where he has come from, how did he contract his disease and what he will be going back to once treatment is concluded. There are three things a good doctor has to be able to do. What are they? The first?

THE FIRST ASSISTANT: Ask questions.

THE SURGEON: The second?

THE SECOND ASSISTANT: Ask questions.

THE SURGEON: And the third?

THE THIRD ASSISTANT: Ask questions, sir.

THE SURGEON: Correct. Ask questions. Particularly concerning ... ?

THE THIRD ASSISTANT: The social conditions, sir.

THE SURGEON: The great thing is never to be shy of looking into the patient's private life – often a regrettably depressing one. If someone is forced to follow some occupation that is bound in the long run to destroy his body, so that he dies in effect to avoid starving to death, one doesn't much like hearing about it and consequently doesn't ask.

He and his followers move on to the new patient.

What has this man got?

The sister whispers in his ear.

Oh, I see.

He gives him a cursory examination with evident reluctance.

Dictates: Contusions on the back and thighs. Open wounds on the abdomen. Further symptoms?

THE SISTER *reads out*: Blood in his urine.

THE SURGEON: Diagnosis on admission?

THE SISTER: Lesion to left kidney.

THE SURGEON: Get him X-rayed. *Starts to turn away.*

THE THIRD ASSISTANT *who has been taking down his medical history*: How was that incurred, sir?

THE SURGEON: What have they put?

THE SISTER: Falling downstairs, it says here.

THE SURGEON *dictating*: A fall down the stairs. Why are his hands tied that way, Sister?

THE SISTER: The patient has twice torn his dressings off, professor.

THE SURGEON: Why?

THE FIRST PATIENT *sotto voce*: Where has the patient come from and where is he going back to?

All heads turn in his direction.

THE SURGEON *clearing his throat*: If this patient seems disturbed give him morphine. *Moves on to the next bed*: Feeling better now? It won't be long before you're fit as a fiddle.

He examines the patient's neck.

ONE ASSISTANT *to another*: Worker. Brought in from Oranienburg.

THE OTHER ASSISTANT *grinning*: Another case of occupational disease, I suppose.

8

The physicists

> Enter the local Newtons
> Dressed up like bearded Teutons –
> Not one of them hook-nosed.
> Their science will end up barbarian
> For they'll get an impeccably Aryan
> State-certified physics imposed.

*Göttingen 1935. Institute for Physics. Two scientists, X and Y.
Y has just entered. He has a conspiratorial look.*

Y: I've got it.

X: What?

Y: The answer to what we asked Mikovsky in Paris.

X: About gravity waves?

Y: Yes.

X: What about it?

Y: Guess who's written giving just what we wanted.

X: Go on.

*Y takes a scrap of paper, writes a name and passes it to X. As
soon as X has read it Y takes it back, tears it into small
pieces and throws it into the stove.*

Y: Mikovsky passed our questions on to him. This is his
answer.

X *grabs for it greedily*: Give me. *He suddenly holds himself
back.* Just suppose we were caught corresponding with him
like this . . .

Y: We absolutely mustn't be.

X: Well, without it we're stuck. Come on, give me.

Y: You won't be able to read it. I used my own shorthand, it's safer. I'll read it out to you.

X: For God's sake be careful.

Y: Is Rollkopf in the lab today? *He points to the right.*

X *pointing to the left*: No, but Reinhardt is. Sit over here.

Y *reads*: The problem concerns two arbitrary countervariant vectors *psi* and *nu* and a countervariant vector *t*. This is used to form the elements of a mixed tensor of the second degree whose structure can be expressed by $\Sigma^{-lr} = C^{-l}_{hr}$.

X *who has been writing this down, suddenly gives him a sign to shut up*: Just a minute.

He gets up and tiptoes over to the wall, left. Having evidently heard nothing suspicious he returns. Y goes on reading aloud, with other similar interruptions. These lead them to inspect the telephone, suddenly open the door etc.

Y: Where matter is passive, incoherent and not acting on itself by means of tensions $T = \mu$ will be the only component of the tensional energy depth that differs from o. Hence a static gravitational field is created whose equation, taking into account the constant proportionality factor $8\pi x$ will be $\Delta f = 4\pi x \mu$. Given a suitable choice of spatial coordinates the degree of variation from $c^2 dt^2$ will be very slight . . .

A door slams somewhere and they try to hide their notes. Then this seems to be unnecessary. From this point on they both become engrossed in the material and apparently oblivious of the danger of what they are doing.

Y *reads on*: . . . by comparison however with the passive mass from which the field originates the masses concerned are very small, and the motion of the bodies implicated in the gravitational field is brought within this static field by means of a geodetic world line. As such this satisfies the variational principle $\delta \int ds = o$ where the ends of the relevant portion of the world line remain fixed.

X: But what's Einstein got to say about . . .

Y's look of horror makes X aware of his mistake so that he sits there paralysed with shock. Y snatches the notes which he has been taking down and hides away all the papers.

Y *very loudly, in the direction of the left-hand wall*: What a typical piece of misplaced Jewish ingenuity. Nothing to do with physics.

Relieved, they again bring out their notes and silently resume work, using the utmost caution.

9

The Jewish wife

Over there we can see men coming
Whom He's forced to relinquish their women
And coupled with blondes in their place.
It's no good their cursing and praying
For once He catches them racially straying
He'll whip them back into the Race.

Frankfurt 1935. It is evening. A woman is packing suitcases. She is choosing what to take. Now and again she removes something from her suitcase and returns it to its original place in the room in order to pack another item instead. For a long while she hesitates whether to take a large photograph of her husband that stands on the chest of drawers. Finally she leaves the picture where it is. The packing tires her and for a time she sits on a suitcase leaning her head on her hand. Then she gets to her feet and telephones.

THE WOMAN: This is Judith Keith. Hullo, is that you, doctor? Good evening. I just wanted to ring up and say you'll have to be looking for another bridge partner; I'm going away. – No, not long, but anyway a few weeks – I want to go to Amsterdam. – Yes, it's said to be lovely there in spring. – I've got friends there. – No, plural, believe it or not. – Who will you get for a fourth? – Come on, we haven't played for a fortnight. – That's right, Fritz had a cold too. It's absurd to go on playing bridge when it's as cold as this, I always say. – But no, doctor, how could I? – Anyway Thekla had her mother there. – I know. – What put that idea into my head? – No, it was nothing sudden, I kept putting it off, and

now I've really got to ... Right, we'll have to cancel our
cinema date, remember me to Thekla. – Ring him up on a
Sunday sometimes, could you perhaps? – Well, au revoir! –
Yes, of course I will. – Goodbye.
She hangs up and calls another number.
This is Judith Keith. Can I speak to Frau Schöck? – Lotte?
– I just wanted to say goodbye. I'm going away for a bit. –
No, nothing's wrong, it's just that I want to see some new
faces. – I really meant to say that Fritz has got the Professor
coming here on Tuesday evening, and I wondered if you
could both come too, I'm off tonight as I said. – Tuesday,
that's it. – No, I only wanted to tell you I'm off tonight,
there's no connection, I just thought you might be able to
come then. – Well, let's say even though I shan't be there,
right? – Yes, I know you're not that sort, but what about it,
these are unsettled times and everybody's being so careful,
so you'll come? – It depends on Max? He'll manage it, the
Professor will be there, tell him. – I must ring off now. –
Goodbye then.
She hangs up and called another number.
That you, Gertrud? It's Judith. I'm so sorry to disturb you.
– Thanks, I just wanted to ask if you could see that Fritz is
all right, I'm going away for a few months. – Being his
sister, I thought you ... Why not? – Nobody'd think that,
anyway not Fritz. – Well, of course he knows we don't ...
get on all that well, but ... Then he can simply call you if
you prefer it that way. – Yes, I'll tell him that. –
Everything's fairly straight, of course the flat's on the big
side. – You'd better leave his workroom to Ida to deal with,
she knows what's to be done. – I find her pretty intelligent,
and he's used to her. – And there's another thing, I hope
you don't mind my saying so, but he doesn't like talking
before meals, can you remember that? I always used to
watch myself. – I don't want to argue about that just now,
it's not long till my train goes and I haven't finished
packing, you know. – Keep an eye on his suits and remind
him to go to his tailor, he's ordered a new overcoat, and do
see that his bedroom's properly heated, he likes sleeping
with the window open and it's too cold. – No, I don't think

he needs to toughen himself up, but I must ring off now. –
I'm very grateful to you, Gertrud, and we'll write to each
other, won't we? – Goodbye.

She hangs up and calls another number.

Anna? It's Judith; look, I'm just off. – No, there's no way
out, things are getting too difficult. – Too difficult! – Well,
no, it isn't Fritz's idea, he doesn't know yet, I simply
packed my things. – I don't think so. – I don't think he'll
say all that much. It's all got too difficult for him, just in
everyday matters. – That's something we haven't arranged.
– We just never talked about it, absolutely never. – No, he
hasn't altered, on the contrary. – I'd be glad if you and Kurt
could look after him a bit, to start with. – Yes, specially
Sundays, and try to make him give up this flat. – It's too big
for him. – I'd like to have come and said goodbye to you,
but it's your porter, you know. – So, goodbye; no, don't
come to the station, it's a bad idea. – Goodbye, I'll write. –
That's a promise.

She hangs up without calling again. She has been smoking.
Now she sets fire to the small book in which she has been
looking up the numbers. She walks up and down two or
three times. Then she starts speaking. She is rehearsing the
short speech which she proposes to make to her husband. It
is evident that he is sitting in a particular chair.

Well, Fritz, I'm off. I suppose I've waited too long, I'm
awfully sorry, but . . .

She stands there thinking, then starts in a different way.

Fritz, you must let me go, you can't keep . . . I'll be your
downfall, it's quite clear; I know you aren't a coward,
you're not scared of the police, but there are worse things.
They won't put you in a camp, but they'll ban you from the
clinic any day now. You won't say anything at the time, but
it'll make you ill. I'm not going to watch you sitting around
the flat pretending to read magazines, it's pure selfishness
on my part, my leaving, that's all. Don't tell me anything . . .

She again stops. She makes a fresh start.

Don't tell me you haven't changed; you have! Only last
week you established quite objectively that the proportion

of Jewish scientists wasn't all that high. Objectivity is always the start of it, and why do you keep telling me I've never been such a Jewish chauvinist as now? Of course I'm one. Chauvinism is catching. Oh, Fritz, what has happened to us?

She again stops. She makes a fresh start.

I never told you I wanted to go away, have done for a long time, because I can't talk when I look at you, Fritz. Then it seems to me there's no point in talkng. It has all been settled already. What's got into them, d'you think? What do they really want? What am I doing to them? I've never had anything to do with politics. Did I vote Communist? But I'm just one of those bourgeois housewives with servants and so on, and now all of a sudden it seems only blondes can be that. I've often thought lately about something you told me years back, how some people were more valuable than others, so one lot were given insulin when they got diabetes and the others weren't. And this was something I understood, idiot that I was. Well, now they've drawn a new distinction of the same sort, and this time I'm one of the less valuable ones. Serves me right.

She again stops. She makes a fresh start.

Yes, I'm packing. Don't pretend you haven't noticed anything the last few days. Nothing really matters, Fritz, except just one thing: if we spend our last hour together without looking at each other's eyes. That's a triumph they can't be allowed, the liars who force everyone else to lie. Ten years ago when somebody said no one would think I was Jewish, you instantly said yes, they would. And that's fine. That was straightforward. Why take things in a roundabout way now? I'm packing so they shan't take away your job as senior physician. And because they've stopped saying good morning to you at the clinic, and because you're not sleeping nowadays. I don't want you to tell me I mustn't go. And I'm hurrying because I don't want to hear you telling me I must. It's a matter of time. Principles are a matter of time. They don't last for ever, any more than a glove does. There are good ones which last a long while. But even they only have a certain life. Don't get the idea that I'm angry. Yes, I am. Why should I always be understanding? What's wrong with the shape of my nose and the colour of my hair? I'm to leave the town where I was born just so they don't have to go short of butter. What sort of people are you, yourself included? You work out the quantum theory and the Trendelenburg test, then allow a lot of semi-barbarians to tell you you're to conquer the world but you can't have the woman you want. The artificial lung, and the dive-bomber! You are monsters or you pander to monsters. Yes, I know I'm being unreasonable, but what good is reason in a world like this? There you sit watching your wife pack and saying nothing. Walls have ears, is that it? But you people say nothing. One lot listens and the other keeps silent. To hell with that. I'm supposed to keep silent too. If I loved you I'd keep silent. I truly do love you. Give me those underclothes. They're suggestive. I'll need them. I'm thirty-six, that isn't too old, but I can't do much more experimenting. The next time I settle in a country things can't be like this. The next man I get must be allowed to keep me. And don't tell me you'll send me money; you know you won't be allowed to. And you aren't to pretend it's just a matter of four weeks either. This business is going to last rather more than four weeks. You know that, and so do I. So don't go telling me 'After all it's only for two or three weeks' as you hand me the fur coat I shan't need till next winter. And don't let's speak about disaster. Let's speak about disgrace. Oh, Fritz!

She stops. A door opens. She hurriedly sees to her appearance. The husband comes in.

THE HUSBAND: What are you doing? Tidying up?

THE WOMAN: No.

THE HUSBAND: Why are you packing?

THE WOMAN: I want to get away.

THE HUSBAND: What are you talking about?

THE WOMAN: We did mention the possibility of my going away for a bit. It's no longer very pleasant here.

THE HUSBAND: That's a lot of nonsense.

THE WOMAN: Do you want me to stay, then?

THE HUSBAND: Where are you thinking of going?

THE WOMAN: Amsterdam. Just away.

THE HUSBAND: But you've got nobody there.

THE WOMAN: No.

THE HUSBAND: Why don't you wish to stay here? There's absolutely no need for you to go so far as I'm concerned.

THE WOMAN: No.

THE HUSBAND: You know I haven't changed, you do, don't you, Judith?

THE WOMAN: Yes.

He embraces her. They stand without speaking among the suitcases.

THE HUSBAND: And there's nothing else makes you want to go?

THE WOMAN: You know that.

THE HUSBAND: It might not be such a bad idea, I suppose. You need a breather. It's stifling in this place. I'll come and collect you. As soon as I get across the frontier, even if it's only for two days, I'll start feeling better.

THE WOMAN: Yes, why don't you?

THE HUSBAND: Things can't go on like this all that much longer. Something's bound to change. The whole business will die down again like an inflammation – it's a disaster, it really is.

THE WOMAN: Definitely. Did you run into Schöck?

THE HUSBAND: Yes, just on the stairs, that's to say. I think he's begun to be sorry about the way they dropped us. He was quite embarrassed. In the long run they can't completely sit on filthy intellectuals like us. And they won't be able to run a war with a lot of spineless wrecks. People aren't all that standoffish if you face up to them squarely. What time are you off, then?

THE WOMAN: Nine-fifteen.

THE HUSBAND: And where am I to send money to?

THE WOMAN: Let's say poste restante, Amsterdam main Post-Office.

THE HUSBAND: I'll see they give me a special permit. Good God, I can't send my wife off with ten marks a month. It's all a lousy business.

THE WOMAN: If you can come and collect me it'll do you a bit
of good.

THE HUSBAND: To read a paper with something in it for once.

THE WOMAN: I rang Gertrud. She'll see you're all right.

THE HUSBAND: Quite unnecessary. For two or three weeks.

THE WOMAN *who has again begun packing*: Do you mind
handing me my fur coat?

THE HUSBAND *handing it to her*: After all it's only for two or
three weeks.

10

The spy

Here come the worthy schoolteachers
The Youth Movement takes the poor creatures
And makes them all thrust out their chest.
Every schoolboy's a spy. So now marking
Is based not on knowledge, but narking
And on who knows whose weaknesses best.

They educate traducers
To set hatchet-men and bruisers
On their own parents' tail.
Denounced by their sons as traitors
To Himmler's apparatus
The fathers go handcuffed to gaol.

*Cologne 1935. A wet Sunday afternoon. The man, the wife
and the boy have finished lunch. The maidservant enters.*

THE MAIDSERVANT: Mr and Mrs Klimbtsch are asking if you
are at home.

THE MAN *snarls*: No.

The maidservant goes out.

THE WIFE: You should have gone to the phone yourself. They
must know we couldn't possibly have gone out yet.

THE MAN: Why couldn't we?

THE WIFE: Because it's raining.

THE MAN: That's no reason.

THE WIFE: Where could we have gone to? That's the first thing they'll ask.

THE MAN: Oh, masses of places.

THE WIFE: Let's go then.

THE MAN: Where to?

THE WIFE: If only it wasn't raining.

THE MAN: And where'd we go if it wasn't raining?

THE WIFE: At least in the old days you could go and meet someone.

Pause.

THE WIFE: It was a mistake you not going to the phone. Now they'll realise we don't want to have them.

THE MAN: Suppose they do?

THE WIFE: Then it wouldn't look very nice, our dropping them just when everyone else does.

THE MAN: We're not dropping them.

THE WIFE: Why shouldn't they come here in that case?

THE MAN: Because Klimbtsch bores me to tears.

THE WIFE: He never bored you in the old days.

THE MAN: In the old days ... All this talk of the old days gets me down.

THE WIFE: Well anyhow you'd never have cut him just because the school inspectors are after him.

THE MAN: Are you telling me I'm a coward?

Pause.

THE MAN: All right, ring up and tell them we've just come back on account of the rain.

The wife remains seated.

THE WIFE: What about asking the Lemkes to come over?

THE MAN: And have them go on telling us we're slack about civil defence?

THE WIFE *to the boy*: Klaus-Heinrich, stop fiddling with the wireless.

The boy turns his attention to the newspapers.

THE MAN: It's a disaster, its raining like this. It's quite

intolerable, living in a country where it's a disaster when it rains.

THE WIFE: Do you really think it's sensible to go round making remarks like that?

THE MAN: I can make what remarks I like between my own four walls. This is my home, and I shall damn well say ... *He is interrupted. The maidservant enters with coffee things. So long as she is present they remain silent.*

THE MAN: Have we got to have a maid whose father is the block warden?

THE WIFE: We've been over that again and again. The last thing you said was that it had its advantages.

THE MAN: What aren't I supposed to have said? If you mentioned anything of the sort to your mother we could land in a proper mess.

THE WIFE: The things I talk about to my mother ...

Enter the maidservant with the coffee.

THE WIFE: That's all right, Erna. You can go now, I'll see to it.

THE MAIDSERVANT: Thank you very much, ma'am.

THE BOY *looking up from his paper*: Is that how vicars always behave, dad?

THE MAN: How do you mean?

THE BOY: Like it says here.

THE MAN: What's that you're reading?

Snatches the paper from his hands.

THE BOY: Hey, our group leader said it was all right for us to know about anything in that paper.

THE MAN: I don't have to go by what your group leader says. It's for me to decide what you can or can't read.

THE WIFE: There's ten pfennigs, Klaus-Heinrich, run over and get yourself something.

THE BOY: But it's raining.

He hangs round the window, trying to make up his mind.

THE MAN: If they go on reporting these cases against priests I shall cancel the paper altogether.

THE WIFE: Which are you going to take, then? They're all reporting them.

THE MAN: If all the papers are full of this kind of filth I'd sooner not read a paper at all. And I wouldn't be any worse informed about what's going on in the world.

THE WIFE: There's something to be said for a bit of a clean-up.

THE MAN: Clean-up, indeed. The whole thing's politics.

THE WIFE: Well, it's none of our business anyway. After all, we're protestants.

THE MAN: It matters to our people all right if it can't hear the word vestry without being reminded of dirt like this.

THE WIFE: But what do you want them to do when this kind of thing happens?

THE MAN: What do I want them to do? Suppose they looked into their own back yard. I'm told it isn't all so snowy white in that Brown House of theirs.

THE WIFE: But that only goes to show how far our people's recovery has gone, Karl.

THE MAN: Recovery! A nice kind of recovery. If that's what recovery looks like, I'd sooner have the disease any day.

THE WIFE: You're so on edge today. Did something happen at the school?

THE MAN: What on earth could have happened at school? And for God's sake don't keep saying I'm on edge, it makes me feel on edge.

THE WIFE: We oughtn't to keep on quarrelling so, Karl. In the old days . . .

THE MAN: Just what I was waiting for. In the old days. Neither in the old days nor now did I wish to have my son's imagination perverted for him.

THE WIFE: Where has he got to, anyway?

THE MAN: How am I to know?

THE WIFE: Did you see him go?

THE MAN: No.

THE WIFE: I can't think where he can have gone. *She calls*: Klaus-Heinrich!
She hurries out of the room, and is heard calling. She returns.

THE WIFE: He really has left.

THE MAN: Why shouldn't he?

THE WIFE: But it's raining buckets.

THE MAN: Why are you so on edge at the boy's having left?

THE WIFE: You remember what we were talking about?

THE MAN: What's that got to do with it?

THE WIFE: You've been so careless lately.

THE MAN: I have certainly not been careless, but even if I had what's that got to do with the boy's having left?

THE WIFE: You know how they listen to everything.

THE MAN: Well?

THE WIFE: Well. Suppose he goes round telling people? You know how they're always dinning it into them in the Hitler Youth. They deliberately encourage the kids to repeat everything. It's so odd his going off so quietly.

THE MAN: Rubbish.

THE WIFE: Didn't you see when he went?

THE MAN: He was hanging round the window for quite a time.

THE WIFE: I'd like to know how much he heard.

THE MAN: But he must know what happens to people who get reported.

THE WIFE: What about that boy the Schmulkes were telling us about? They say his father's still in a concentration camp. I wish we knew how long he was in the room.

THE MAN: The whole thing's a load of rubbish.

He hastens to the other rooms and calls the boy.

THE WIFE: I just can't see him going off somewhere without saying a word. It wouldn't be like him.

THE MAN: Mightn't he be with a school friend?

THE WIFE: Then he'd have to be at the Mummermanns'. I'll give them a ring. *She telephones.*

THE MAN: It's all a false alarm, if you ask me.

THE WIFE *telephoning*: Is that Mrs Mummermann? It's Mrs Furcke here. Good afternoon. Is Klaus-Heinrich with you? He isn't? – Then where on earth can the boy be? – Mrs Mummermann do you happen to know if the Hitler Youth place is open on Sunday afternoons? – It is? – Thanks a lot, I'll ask them.

She hangs up. They sit in silence.

THE MAN: What do you think he overheard?

THE WIFE: You were talking about the paper. You shouldn't
have said what you did about the Brown House. He's so
patriotic about that kind of thing.

THE MAN: What am I supposed to have said about the Brown
House?

THE WIFE: You remember perfectly well. That things weren't
all snowy white in there.

THE MAN: Well, nobody can take that as an attack, can they?
Saying things aren't all white, or snowy white rather, as I
qualified it – which makes a difference, quite a substantial
one at that – well, it's more a kind of jocular remark like the
man in the street makes in the vernacular, sort of, and all it
really means is that probably not absolutely everything
even there is always exactly as the Führer would like it to
be. I quite deliberately emphasised that this was only
'probably' so by using the phrase, as I very well remember,
'I'm *told*' things aren't *all* – and that's another obvious
qualification – so snowy white there. 'I'm told'; that doesn't
mean it's necessarily so. How could I say things aren't
snowy white? I haven't any proof. Wherever there are
human beings there are imperfections. That's all I was
suggesting, and in very qualified form. And in any case
there was a certain occasion when the Führer himself
expressed the same kind of criticisms a great deal more
strongly.

THE WIFE: I don't understand you. You don't need to talk to
me in that way.

THE MAN: I'd like to think I don't. I wish I knew to what
extent you gossip about all that's liable to be said between
these four walls in the heat of the moment. Of course I
wouldn't dream of accusing you of casting ill-considered
aspersions on your husband, any more than I'd think my
boy capable for one moment of doing anything to harm his
own father. But doing harm and doing it wittingly are
unfortunately two very different matters.

THE WIFE: You can stop that right now! What about the kind
of things you say yourself? Here am I worrying myself silly
whether you make that remark about life in Nazi Germany

being intolerable before or after the one about the Brown House.

THE MAN: I never said anything of the sort.

THE WIFE: You're acting absolutely as if I were the police. All I'm doing is racking my brains about what the boy may have overheard.

THE MAN: The term Nazi Germany just isn't in my vocabulary.

THE WIFE: And that stuff about the warden of our block and how the papers print nothing but lies, and what you were saying about civil defence the other day – when does the boy hear a single constructive remark? That just doesn't do any good to a child's attitude of mind, it's simply demoralising, and at a time when the Führer keeps stressing that Germany's future lies in Germany's youth. He really isn't the kind of boy to rush off and denounce one just like that. It makes me feel quite ill.

THE MAN: He's vindictive, though.

THE WIFE: What on earth has he got to be vindictive about?

THE MAN: God knows, but there's bound to be something. The time I confiscated his tree-frog perhaps.

THE WIFE: But that was a week ago.

THE MAN: It's that kind of thing that sticks in his mind, though.

THE WIFE: What did you confiscate it for, anyway?

THE MAN: Because he wouldn't catch any flies for it. He was letting the creature starve.

THE WIFE: He really is run off his feet, you know.

THE MAN: There's not much the frog can do about that.

THE WIFE: But he never came back to the subject, and I gave him ten pfennigs only a moment ago. He only has to want something and he gets it.

THE MAN: Exactly. I call that bribery.

THE WIFE: What do you mean by that?

THE MAN: They'll simply say we were trying to bribe him to keep his mouth shut.

THE WIFE: What do you imagine they could do to you?

THE MAN: Absolutely anything. There's no limit. My God!

And to think I'm supposed to be a teacher. An educator of our youth. Our youth scares me stiff.

THE WIFE: But they've nothing against you.

THE MAN: They've something against everyone. Everyone's suspect. Once the suspicion's there, one's suspect.

THE WIFE: But a child's not a reliable witness. A child hasn't the faintest idea what it's talking about.

THE MAN: So you say. But when did they start having to have witnesses for things?

THE WIFE: Couldn't we work out what you could have meant by your remarks? Then he could just have misunderstood you.

THE MAN: Well, what did I say? I can't even remember. It's all the fault of that damned rain. It puts one in a bad mood. Actually I'm the last person to say anything against the moral resurgence the German people is going through these days. I foresaw the whole thing as early as the winter of 1932.

THE WIFE: Karl, there just isn't time to discuss that now. We must straighten everything out right away. There's not a minute to spare.

THE MAN: I don't believe Karl-Heinrich's capable of it.

THE WIFE: Let's start with the Brown House and all the filth.

THE MAN: I never said a word about filth.

THE WIFE: You said the paper's full of filth and you want to cancel it.

THE MAN: Right, the paper. But not the Brown House.

THE WIFE: Couldn't you have been saying that you won't stand for such filth in the churches? And that you think the people now being tried could quite well be the same as used to spread malicious rumours about the Brown House suggesting things weren't all that snowy white there? And that they ought to have started looking into their own place instead? And what you were telling the boy was that he should stop fiddling with the wireless and read the paper because you're firmly of the opinion that the youth of the Third Reich should have a clear view of what's happening round about them.

THE MAN: It wouldn't be any use.

THE WIFE: Karl, you're not to give up now. You should be strong, like the Führer keeps on . . .

THE MAN: I'm not going to be brought before the law and have my own flesh and blood standing in the witness box and giving evidence against me.

THE WIFE: There's no need to take it like that.

THE MAN: It was a great mistake our seeing so much of the Klimbtsches.

THE WIFE: But nothing whatever has happened to him.

THE MAN: Yes, but there's talk of an inquiry.

THE WIFE: What would it be like if everybody got in such a panic as soon as there was talk of an inquiry?

THE MAN: Do you think our block warden has anything against us?

THE WIFE: You mean, supposing they asked him? He got a box of cigars for his birthday the other day and his Christmas box was ample.

THE MAN: The Gauffs gave him fifteen marks.

THE WIFE: Yes, but they were still taking the socialist paper in 1932, and as late as May 1933 they were hanging out the old nationalist flag.

The phone rings.

THE MAN: That's the phone.

THE WIFE: Shall I answer it?

THE MAN: I don't know.

THE WIFE: Who could be ringing us?

THE MAN: Wait a moment. If it rings again, answer it.

They wait. It doesn't ring again.

THE MAN: We can't go on living like this!

THE WIFE: Karl!

THE MAN: A Judas, that's what you've borne me. Sitting at the table listening, gulping down the soup we've given him and noting down whatever his father says, the little spy.

THE WIFE: That's a dreadful thing to say.

Pause.

THE WIFE: Do you think we ought to make any kind of preparations?

THE MAN: Do you think he'll bring them straight back with him?

THE WIFE: Could he really?

THE MAN: Perhaps I'd better put on my Iron Cross.

THE WIFE: Of course you must, Karl.

He gets it and puts it on with shaking hands.

THE WIFE: But they've nothing against you at school, have they?

THE MAN: How's one to tell? I'm prepared to teach whatever they want taught; but what's that? If only I could tell ... How am I to know what they want Bismarck to have been like? When they're taking so long to publish the new text books. Couldn't you give the maid another ten marks? She's another who's always listening.

THE WIFE *nodding*: And what about the picture of Hitler; shouldn't we hang it above your desk? It'd look better.

THE MAN: Yes, do that.

The wife starts taking down the picture.

THE MAN: Suppose the boy goes and says we deliberately rehung it, though, it might look as if we had a bad conscience.

The wife puts the picture back on its old hook.

THE MAN: Wasn't that the door?

THE WIFE: I didn't hear anything.

THE MAN: It was.

THE WIFE: Karl!

She embraces him.

THE MAN: Keep a grip on yourself. Pack some things for me.

The door of the flat opens. Man and wife stand rigidly side by side in the corner of the room. The door opens and enter the boy, a paper bag in his hand. Pause.

THE BOY: What's the matter with you people?

THE WIFE: Where have you been?

The boy shows her the bag, which contains chocolate.

THE WIFE: Did you simply go out to buy chocolate?

THE BOY: Whatever else? Obvious, isn't it?

He crosses the room munching, and goes out. His parents look enquiringly after him.

THE MAN: Do you suppose he's telling the truth?
The wife shrugs her shoulders.

11

The black shoes

> These widows and orphans you're seeing
> Have heard Him guaranteeing
> A great time by and by.
> Meanwhile they must make sacrifices
> As the shops all put up their prices.
> That great time is pie in the sky.

Bitterfeld, 1935. Kitchen in a working-class flat. The mother is peeling potatoes. Her thirteen-year-old daughter is doing homework.

THE DAUGHTER: Mum, am I getting my two pfennigs?
THE MOTHER: For the Hitler Youth?
THE DAUGHTER: Yes.
THE MOTHER: I haven't any money left.
THE DAUGHTER: But if I don't bring my two pfennigs a week I won't be going to the country this summer. And our teacher said Hitler wants town and country to get to know each other. Town people are supposed to get closer to the farmers. But I'll have to bring along my two pfennigs.
THE MOTHER: I'll try to find some way of letting you have them.
THE DAUGHTER: Oh lovely, Mum. I'll give a hand with the 'taters. It's lovely in the country, isn't it? Proper meals there. Our gym teacher was saying I've got a potato belly.
THE MOTHER: You've nothing of the kind.
THE DAUGHTER: Not right now. Last year I had. A bit.
THE MOTHER: I might be able to get us some offal.
THE DAUGHTER: I get my roll at school; that's more than you do. Bertha was saying when she went to the country last

year they had bread and goose dripping. Meat too sometimes. Lovely, isn't it?

THE MOTHER: Of course.

THE DAUGHTER: And all that fresh air.

THE MOTHER: Didn't she have to do some work too?

THE DAUGHTER: Of course. But lots to eat. Only the farmer
was a nuisance, she said.

THE MOTHER: What'd he do?

THE DAUGHTER: Oh, nothing. Just kept pestering her.

THE MOTHER: Aha.

THE DAUGHTER: Bertha's bigger than me, though. A year
older.

THE MOTHER: Get on with your homework.

Pause, then:

THE DAUGHTER: But I won't have to wear those old black
shoes from the welfare, will I?

THE MOTHER: You won't be needing them. You've got your
other pair, haven't you?

THE DAUGHTER: Just that those have got a hole.

THE MOTHER: Oh dear, when it's so wet.

THE DAUGHTER: I'll put some paper in, that'll do it.

THE MOTHER: No, it won't. If they've gone they'll have to be
resoled.

THE DAUGHTER: That's so expensive.

THE MOTHER: What've you got against the welfare pair?

THE DAUGHTER: I can't stand them.

THE MOTHER: Because they look so clumsy?

THE DAUGHTER: So you think so too.

THE MOTHER: Of course they're older.

THE DAUGHTER: Have I *got* to wear them?

THE MOTHER: If you can't stand them you needn't wear
them.

THE DAUGHTER: I'm not being vain, am I?

THE MOTHER: No. Just growing up.

Pause, then:

THE DAUGHTER: Then can I have my two pfennigs, Mum?
I do so want to go.

THE MOTHER *slowly*: I haven't the money for that.

12

Labour service

> By sweeping away class barriers
> The poor are made fetchers and carriers
> In Hitler's Labour Corps.
> The rich serve a year alongside them
> To show that no conflicts divide them.
> Some pay would please them more.

The Lüneburger Heide, 1935. A Labour Service column at work. A young worker and a student are digging together.

THE STUDENT: What did they put that stocky little fellow from Column 3 in clink for?

THE YOUNG WORKER *grinning*: The group leader was saying we'll learn what it's like to work and he said, under his breath like, he'd as soon learn what it's like to get a pay packet. They weren't pleased.

THE STUDENT: Why say something like that?

THE YOUNG WORKER: Because he already knows what it's like to work, I should think. He was down the pits at fourteen.

THE STUDENT: Look out, Tubby's coming.

THE YOUNG WORKER: If he looks our way I can't just dig out half a spit.

THE STUDENT: But I can't shovel away more than I'm doing.

THE YOUNG WORKER: If he cops me there'll be trouble.

THE STUDENT: No more cigarettes from me, then.

THE YOUNG WORKER: He'll cop me sure enough.

THE STUDENT: And you want to go on leave, don't you? Think I'm going to pay you if you can't take a little risk like that?

THE YOUNG WORKER: You've already had your money's worth and more.

THE STUDENT: But I'm not going to pay you.

THE GROUP LEADER *comes and watches them*: Well, Herr Doktor, now you can see what working is really like, can't you?

THE STUDENT: Yes, Herr Group Leader.
The young worker digs half a spit of earth. The student pretends to be shovelling like mad.
THE GROUP LEADER: You owe it all to the Führer.
THE STUDENT: Yes, Herr Group Leader.
THE GROUP LEADER: Shoulder to shoulder and no class barriers; that's his way. The Führer wants no distinctions made in his labour camps. Never mind who your dad is. Carry on! *He goes.*
THE STUDENT: I don't call that half a spit.
THE YOUNG WORKER: Well, I do.
THE STUDENT: No cigarettes for today. Better remember there are an awful lot of people want cigarettes just as much as you.
THE YOUNG WORKER *slowly*: Yes, there are an awful lot of people like me. That's something we often forget.

13
Workers' playtime

Then the media, a travelling circus
Come to interview the workers
With microphone in hand
But the workers can't be trusted
So the interview is adjusted
To fit what Goebbels has planned.

Leipzig 1934. Foreman's office in a factory. A radio announcer bearing a microphone is chatting to three workers; a middle-aged worker, an old worker and a woman worker. In the background are a gentleman from the office and a stocky figure in SA uniform.

THE ANNOUNCER: Here we are with flywheels and driving belts in full swing all around us, surrounded by our comrades working as busily as ants, joyously doing their bit to provide our beloved fatherland with everything it requires. This morning we are visiting the Fuchs spinning mills. And in spite of the hard toil and the tensing of every muscle here we see nothing but joyous and contented faces on all sides. But let us get our comrades to speak for themselves. *To the old worker*: I understand you've been working here for twenty-one years, Mr . . .

THE OLD WORKER: Sedelmaier.

THE ANNOUNCER: Mr Sedelmaier. Tell me, Mr Sedelmaier, how is it that we see nothing but these happy, joyous faces on every side?

THE OLD WORKER *after a moment's thought*: There's a lot of jokes told.

THE ANNOUNCER: Really? Right, so a cheerful jest or two makes work seem child's play, what? The deadly menace of pessimism is unknown under National Socialism, you mean. Different in the old days, wasn't it?

THE OLD WORKER: Aye.

THE ANNOUNCER: That rotten old Weimar republic didn't give the workers much to laugh about you mean. What are we working for, they used to ask.

THE OLD WORKER: Aye, that's what some of them say.

THE ANNOUNCER: I didn't quite get that. Oh, I see, you're referring to the inevitable grouses, but they're dying out now they see that kind of thing's a waste of time because everything's booming in the Third Reich now there's a strong hand on the helm once again. That's what you feel too – *to the woman worker* – isn't it, Miss . . .

THE WOMAN WORKER: Schmidt.

THE ANNOUNCER: Miss Schmidt. And which of these steel mammoths enjoys your services?

THE WOMAN WORKER *reciting*: And then we also work at decorating our place of work which gives us great pleasure. Our portrait of the Führer was purchased thanks to voluntary contributions and we are very proud of him. Also of the geranium plants which provide a magical touch of colour in the greyness of our working environment, by suggestion of Miss Kinze.

THE ANNOUNCER: So you decorate your place of work with flowers, the sweet offspring of the fields. And I imagine there've been a good few other changes in this factory since Germany's destiny took its new turning?

GENTLEMAN FROM THE OFFICE *prompting*: Wash rooms.

THE WOMAN WORKER: The wash rooms were the personal idea of Mr Bäuschle our managing director for which we would like to express our heartfelt thanks. Anybody who wants to wash can do so in these fine washrooms so long as there isn't too much of a crowd fighting for the basins.

THE ANNOUNCER: Everybody wants to be first, what? So there's always a jolly throng?

THE WOMAN WORKER: Only six taps for 552 of us. So there are lots of quarrels. It's disgraceful how some of them behave.

THE ANNOUNCER: But it's all sorted out perfectly happily. And now we are going to hear a few words from Mr – if you'd be so good as to tell me your name?

THE WORKER: Mahn.

THE ANNOUNCER: Mr Mahn. Right, Mr Mahn, would you tell us what moral effect the great increase in the workforce here has had on your fellow workers?

THE WORKER: How do you mean?

THE ANNOUNCER: Well, are all of you happy to see the wheels turning and plenty of work for everybody?

THE WORKER: You bet.

THE ANNOUNCER: And everybody once more able to take his wage packet home at the end of the week, that's not to be sneezed at either.

THE WORKER: No.

THE ANNOUNCER: Things weren't always like that. Under that rotten old republic many a comrade had to plod his weary way to the public welfare and live on charity.

THE WORKER: 18 marks 50. No deductions.

THE ANNOUNCER *with a forced laugh*: Ha. Ha. A capital joke! Not much to deduct, was there?

THE WORKER: No. Nowadays they deduct more.

The gentleman from the office moves forward uneasily, as does the stocky man in SA uniform.

THE ANNOUNCER: So there we are, everybody's once again got bread and work under National Socialism. You're absolutely right, Mr – what did you say your name was? Not a single wheel is idle, not a single shaft needs to rust up in Adolf Hitler's Germany. *He roughly pushes the worker away from the microphone.* In joyful cooperation the intellectual worker and the manual worker are tackling the reconstruction of our beloved German Fatherland. Heil Hitler!

14
The box

> The coffins the SA carry
> Are sealed up tight, to bury
> Their victims' raw remains.
> Here's one who wouldn't give in
> He fought for better living
> That we might lose our chains.

Essen 1934. Working-class flat. A woman with two children. A young worker and his wife, who are calling on them. The woman is weeping. Steps can be heard on the staircase. The door is open.

THE WOMAN: He simply said they were paying starvation wages, that's all. And it's true. What's more, our elder girl's got lung trouble and we can't afford milk. They couldn't possibly have harmed him, could they?
The SA men bring in a big box and put it on the floor.

SA MAN: Don't make a song and dance about it. Anybody can catch pneumonia. Here are the papers, all present and correct. And don't you go doing anything silly, now.
The SA men leave.

A CHILD: Mum, is Dad in there?

THE WORKER *who has gone over to the box*: That's zinc it's made of.

THE CHILD: Please can we open it?

THE WORKER *in a rage*: You bet we can. Where's your toolbox?

THE YOUNG WOMAN: Don't you open it, Hans. It'll only make them come for you.

THE WORKER: I want to see what they did to him. They're frightened of people seeing that. That's why they used zinc. Leave me alone!

THE YOUNG WOMAN: I'm not leaving you alone. Didn't you hear them?

THE WORKER: Don't you think we ought to just have a look at him?

THE WOMAN *taking her children by the hand and going up to the zinc box*: There's still my brother, they might come for him, Hans. And they might come for you too. The box can stay shut. We don't need to see him. He won't be forgotten.

15
Release

Questioned in torture cellars
These men were no tale-tellers.
They held out all through the night.
Let's hope they didn't go under
But their wives and friends must wonder
What took place at first light.

Berlin, 1936. Working-class kitchen. Sunday morning. Man and wife. Sound of military music in the distance.

THE MAN: He'll be here any minute.

THE WIFE: None of you know anything against him, after all.

THE MAN: All we know is that they let him out of the concentration camp.

THE WIFE: So why don't you trust him?

THE MAN: There've been too many cases. They put so much pressure on them in there.

THE WIFE: How's he to convince you?

THE MAN: We'll find out where he stands all right.

THE WIFE: Might take time.

THE MAN: Yes.

THE WIFE: And he might be a first-rate comrade.

THE MAN: He might.

THE WIFE: It must be dreadful for him when he sees everybody mistrusting him.

THE MAN: He knows it's necessary.

THE WIFE: All the same.

THE MAN: I can hear something. Don't go away while we're talking.

There is a ring. The man opens the door, the released man enters.

THE MAN: Hullo, Max.

The released man silently shakes hands with the man and his wife.

THE WIFE: Would you like a cup of coffee with us? We're just going to have some.

THE RELEASED MAN: If it's not too much trouble.

Pause.

THE RELEASED MAN: You got a new cupboard.

THE WIFE: It's really an old one, cost eleven marks fifty. Ours was falling to pieces.

THE RELEASED MAN: Ha.

THE MAN: Anything doing in the street?

THE RELEASED MAN: They're collecting.

THE WIFE: We could do with a suit for Willi.

THE MAN: Hey, I'm not out of work.

THE WIFE: That's just why we could do with a suit for you.

THE MAN: Don't talk such nonsense.

THE RELEASED MAN: Work or no work, anybody can do with something.

THE MAN: You found work yet?

THE RELEASED MAN: They say so.

THE MAN: At Seimens?

THE RELEASED MAN: There or some other place.

THE MAN: It's not as hard as it was.

THE RELEASED MAN: No.

Pause.

THE MAN: How long you been inside?

THE RELEASED MAN: Six months.

THE MAN: Meet anyone in there?

THE RELEASED MAN: No one I knew. *Pause.* They're sending them to different camps these days. You could land up in Bavaria.

THE MAN: Ha.

THE RELEASED MAN: Things haven't changed much outside.

THE MAN: Not so as you'd notice.

THE WIFE: We live a very quiet life, you know. Willi hardly ever sees any of his old friends, do you, Willi?

THE MAN: Ay, we keep pretty much to ourselves.

THE RELEASED MAN: I don't suppose you ever got them to shift those rubbish bins from the hallway?

THE WIFE: Goodness, you remember that? Ay, he says he can't find anywhere else for them.

THE RELEASED MAN *as the wife is pouring him a cup of coffee*: Just give me a drop. I don't want to stay long.

THE MAN: Got any plans?

THE RELEASED MAN: Selma told me you looked after her when she was laid up. Thanks very much.

THE WIFE: It was nothing. We'd have told her to come over in the evening more, only we've not even got the wireless.

THE MAN: Anything they tell you is in the paper anyway.

THE RELEASED MAN: Not that there's much in the old rag.

THE WIFE: As much as there is in the *Völkischer Beobachter*, though.

THE RELEASED MAN: And in the *Völkischer Beobachter* there's just as much as there is in the old rag, eh?

THE MAN: I don't read that much in the evenings. Too tired.

THE WIFE: Here, what's wrong with your hand? All screwed up like that and two fingers missing?

THE RELEASED MAN: Oh, I had a fall.

THE MAN: Good thing it was your left one.

THE RELEASED MAN: Ay, that was a bit of luck. I'd like a word with you. No offence meant, Mrs Mahn.

THE WIFE: None taken. I've just got to clean the stove.

She gets to work on the stove. The released man watches her, a thin smile on his lips.

THE MAN: We've got to go out right after dinner. Has Selma quite recovered?

THE RELEASED MAN: All but for her hip. Doing washing is bad for her. Tell me ... *He stops short and looks at them. They look at him. He says nothing further.*

THE MAN *hoarsely*: What about a walk round the Alexanderplatz before dinner? See what's doing with their collection?

THE WIFE: We could do that, couldn't we?

THE RELEASED MAN: Sure.

Pause.

THE RELEASED MAN *quietly*: Hey, Willi, you know I've not changed.

THE MAN *lightly*: Course you haven't. They might have a band playing there. Get yourself ready, Anna. We've finished our coffee. I'll just run a comb through my hair. *They go into the next room. The released man remains seated. He has picked up his hat. He is aimlessly whistling. The couple return, dressed to go out.*

THE MAN: Come on then, Max.

THE RELEASED MAN: Very well. But let me just say: I find it entirely right.

THE MAN: Good, then let's go.

They go out together.

16

Charity begins at home

> With banners and loud drumming
> The Winter Aid come slumming
> Into the humblest door.
> They've marched round and collected
> The crumbs the rich have rejected
> And brought them to the poor.
>
> Their hands, more used to beatings
> Now offer gifts and greetings.
> They conjure up a smile.

Their charity soon crashes
Their food all turns to ashes
And chokes the uttered 'Heil!'

Karlsruhe 1937. An old woman's flat. She is standing at a table with her daughter while the two SA men deliver a parcel from the Winter Aid Organisation.

THE FIRST SA MAN: Here you are, Ma, a present from the Führer.

THE SECOND SA MAN: So you can't say he's not looking after you properly.

THE OLD WOMAN: Thanks very much, thanks very much. Look, Erna, potatoes. And a woollen sweater. And apples.

THE FIRST SA MAN: And a letter from the Führer with something in it. Go on, open it.

THE OLD WOMAN *opening the letter:* Five marks! What d'you say to that, Erna?

THE SECOND SA MAN: Winter Aid.

THE OLD WOMAN: You must take an apple, young man, and you too, for bringing these things to me, and up all those stairs too. It's all I got to offer you. And I'll take one myself.
She takes a bite at an apple. All eat apples with the exception of the young woman.

THE OLD WOMAN: Go on, Erna, you take one too, don't just stand there. That shows you things aren't like your husband says.

THE FIRST SA MAN: What does he say, then?

THE YOUNG WOMAN: He doesn't say anything. The old lady's wandering.

THE OLD WOMAN: Of course it's just his way of talking, you know, it don't mean any harm, just the way they all talk. How prices have gone up a bit much lately. *Pointing at her daughter with the apple:* And she got her account book and actually reckoned food had cost her 123 marks more this year than last. Didn't you, Erna? *She notices that the SA man seems to have taken this amiss.* But of course it's just because we're rearming, isn't it? What's the matter, I said something wrong?

THE FIRST SA MAN: Where do you keep your account book, young woman?

THE SECOND SA MAN: And who are you in the habit of showing it to?

THE YOUNG WOMAN: It's at home. I don't show it to no one.

THE OLD WOMAN: You can't object if she keeps accounts, how could you?

THE FIRST SA MAN: And if she goes about spreading alarm and despondency, are we allowed to object then?

THE SECOND SA MAN: What's more I don't remember her saying 'Heil Hitler' all that loudly when we came in. Do you?

THE OLD WOMAN: But she *did* say 'Heil Hitler' and I say the same. 'Heil Hitler'!

THE SECOND SA MAN: Nice nest of Marxists we've stumbled on here, Albert. We'd better have a good look at those accounts. Just you come along and show us where you live. *He seizes the young woman by the arm.*

THE OLD WOMAN: But she's in her third month. You can't ... that's no way for you to behave. After bringing the parcel and taking the apples. Erna! But she *did* say 'Heil Hitler', what am I do do, Heil Hitler! Heil Hitler! *She vomits up the apple. The SA lead her daughter off.*

THE OLD WOMAN *continuing to vomit*: Heil Hitler!

17
Two bakers

Now come the master bakers
Compelled to act as fakers
And made to use their art
On substitute ingredients –
Spuds, bran and blind obedience.
It lands them in the cart.

Landsberg, 1936. Prison yard. Prisoners are walking in a

circle. Now and again two of them talk quietly to each other downstage.

THE ONE: So you're a baker too, new boy?
THE OTHER: Yes. Are you?
THE ONE: Yes. What did they get you for?
THE OTHER: Look out!
  They again walk round the circle.
THE OTHER: Refusing to mix potatoes and bran in my bread. And you? How long've you been in?
THE ONE: Two years.
THE OTHER: And what did they get you for? Look out!
  They again walk round the circle.
THE ONE: Mixing bran in my bread. Two years ago they still called that adulteration.
THE OTHER: Look out!

18

The farmer feeds his sow

> You'll notice in our procession
> The farmer's sour expression:
> They've underpriced his crop.
> But what his pigs require
> Is milk, whose price has gone higher.
> It makes him blow his top.

Aichach, 1937. A farmyard. It is night. The farmer is standing by the pigsty giving instructions to his wife and two children.

THE FARMER: I wasn't having you mixed up in this, but you found out and now you'll just have to shut your trap. Or else your dad'll go off to Landsberg gaol for the rest of his born days. There's nowt wrong in our feeding our cattle when they're hungry. God doesn't want any beast to starve. And soon as she's hungry she squeals and I'm not having a sow squealing with hunger on my farm. But they won't let me feed her. Cause the State says so. But I'm feeding her just the same, I am. Cause if I don't feed her she'll die on me, and I shan't get any compensation for that.

THE FARMER'S WIFE: Too right. Our grain's our grain. And those buggers have no business telling us what to do. They got the Jews out but the State's the worst Jew of them all. And the Reverend Father saying 'Thou shalt not muzzle the ox that treadeth out the corn.' That's his way of telling us go ahead and feed our cattle. It weren't us as made their four-year plan, and we weren't asked.

THE FARMER: That's right. They don't favour the farmers and the farmers don't favour them. I'm supposed to deliver over my grain and pay through the nose for my cattle feed. So that that spiv can buy guns.

THE FARMER'S WIFE: You stand by the gate, Toni, and you, Marie, run into the pasture and soon as you see anyone coming give us a call.

The children take up their positions. The farmer mixes his pig-swill and carries it to the sty, looking cautiously around him. His wife looks cautiously too.

THE FARMER *pouring the swill into the sow's trough*: Go on, have a good feed, love. Heil Hitler! When a beast's hungry there ain't no State.

19
The old militant

Behold several million electors.
One hundred per cent in all sectors
Have asked to be led by the nose.
They didn't get real bread and butter
They didn't get warm coats or fodder
They *did* get the leader they chose.

Calw (Württemberg), 1938. A square with small shops. In the background a butcher's, in the foreground a dairy. It is a dark winter's morning. The butcher's is not open yet. But the dairy's lights are on and there are a few customers waiting.

A PETIT-BOURGEOIS: No butter again today, what?

THE WOMAN: It'll be all I can afford on my old man's pay, anyway.

A YOUNG FELLOW: Stop grumbling, will you? Germany needs guns, not butter, no question about that. He spelled it out.

THE WOMAN *backing down*: Quite right too.
Silence.

THE YOUNG FELLOW: D'you think we could have reoccupied the Rhineland with butter? Everyone was for doing it the way we did, but catch them making any sacrifices.

A SECOND WOMAN: Keep your hair on. All of us are making some.

THE YOUNG FELLOW *mistrustfully*: What d'you mean?

THE SECOND WOMAN *to the first*: Don't you give something when they come round collecting?
The first woman nods.

THE SECOND WOMAN: There you are. She's giving. And so are we. Voluntary-like.

THE YOUNG FELLOW: That's an old story. Not a penny to spare when the Führer needs a bit of backing, as it were, for his mighty tasks. It's just rags, what they give the Winter Aid. They'd give 'em the moths if they could get away with it. We know the kind we got to deal with. That factory owner in number twelve went and gave us a pair of worn-out riding boots.

THE PETIT-BOURGEOIS: No foresight, that's the trouble.
The dairywoman comes out of her shop in a white apron.

THE DAIRYWOMAN: Won't be long now. *To the second woman*: Morning, Mrs Ruhl. Did you hear they came for young Lettner last night?

THE SECOND WOMAN: What, the butcher?

THE DAIRYWOMAN: Right, his son.

THE SECOND WOMAN: But he was in the SA.

THE DAIRYWOMAN: Used to be. The old fellow's been in the party since 1929. He was away at a livestock sale yesterday or they'd have taken him off too.

THE SECOND WOMAN: What're they supposed to have done?

THE DAIRYWOMAN: Been overcharging for meat. He was

hardly getting nothing on his quota and had to turn customers away. Then they say he started buying on the black market. From the Jews even.

THE YOUNG FELLOW: Bound to come for him, weren't they?

THE DAIRYWOMAN: Used to be one of the keenest of the lot, he did. He shopped old Zeisler at number seventeen for not taking the *Völkischer Beobachter*. An old militant, that's him.

THE SECOND WOMAN: He'll get a surprise when he comes back.

THE DAIRYWOMAN: *If* he comes back.

THE PETIT-BOURGEOIS: No foresight, that's the trouble.

THE SECOND WOMAN: Looks as if they won't open at all today.

THE DAIRYWOMAN: Best thing they can do. The police only have to look round a place like that and they're bound to find something, aren't they? With stock so hard to get. We get ours from the cooperative, no worries so far. *Calling out*: There'll be no cream today. *General murmur of disappointment*. They say Lettner's raised a mortgage on the house. They counted on its being cancelled or something.

THE PETIT-BOURGEOIS: They can't start cancelling mortgages. That'd be going a bit too far.

THE SECOND WOMAN: Young Lettner was quite a nice fellow.

THE DAIRYWOMAN: Old Lettner was always the crazy one. Went and shoved the boy in the SA, just like that. When he'd sooner have been going out with a girl, if you ask me.

THE YOUNG FELLOW: What d'you mean, crazy?

THE DAIRYWOMAN: Crazy, did I say? Oh, he always went crazy if anyone said anything against the Idea, in the old days. He was always speaking about the Idea, and down with the selfishness of the individual.

THE PETIT-BOURGEOIS: They're opening up, after all.

THE SECOND WOMAN: Got to live, haven't they?

A stout woman comes out of the butcher's shop, which is now half-lit. She stops on the pavement and looks down the street for something. Then she turns to the dairywoman.

THE BUTCHER'S WIFE: Good morning, Mrs Schlichter. Have

you seen our Richard? He should have been here with the
meat well before now.

*The dairywoman doesn't reply. All of them just stare at her.
She understands, and goes quickly back into the shop.*

THE DAIRYWOMAN: Act as though nothing's happened. It all
blew up day before yesterday when the old man made such
a stink you could hear him shouting right across the square.
They counted that against him.

THE SECOND WOMAN: I never heard a word about that, Mrs
Schlichter.

THE DAIRYWOMAN: Really? Didn't you know how he
refused to hang that plaster ham they brought him in his
shop window? He'd gone and ordered it cause they
insisted, what with him hanging nothing in his window all
week but the slate with the prices. He said: I've got nothing
left for the window. When they brought that dummy ham,
along with a side of veal, what's more, so natural you'd
think it was real, he shouted he wasn't hanging any make-
believe stuff in his window as well as a lot more I wouldn't
care to repeat. Against the government, all of it, after which
he threw the stuff into the road. They had to pick it up out
of the dirt.

THE SECOND WOMAN: Ts, ts, ts, ts.

THE PETIT-BOURGEOIS: No foresight, that's the trouble.

THE SECOND WOMAN: How can people lose control like that?

THE DAIRYWOMAN: Particularly such a smooth operator.

*At this moment someone turns on a second light in the
butcher's shop.*

THE DAIRYWOMAN: Look at that!

She points excitedly at the half-lit shop window.

THE SECOND WOMAN: There's something in the window.

THE DAIRYWOMAN: It's old Lettner. In his coat too. But
what's he standing on? *Suddenly calls out*: Mrs Lettner!

THE BUTCHER'S WIFE: What is it?

*The dairywoman points speechlessly at the shop window.
The butcher's wife glances at it, screams and falls down in a
faint. The second woman and the dairywoman hurry over
to her.*

THE SECOND WOMAN *back over her shoulder*: He's hung himself in his shop window.

THE PETIT-BOURGEOIS: There's a sign round his neck.

THE FIRST WOMAN: It's the slate. There's something written on it.

THE SECOND WOMAN: It says 'I voted for Hitler'.

20

The Sermon on the Mount

> The Church's Ten Commandments
> Are subject to amendments
> By order of the police.
> Her broken head is bleeding
> For new gods are succeeding
> Her Jewish god of peace.

Lübeck 1937. A fisherman's kitchen. The fisherman is dying. By his bed stand his wife and, in SA uniform, his son. The pastor is there.

THE DYING MAN: Tell me: is there really anything afterwards?

THE PASTOR: Are you then troubled by doubts?

THE WIFE: He's kept on saying these last four days that there's so much talking and promising you don't know what to believe. You mustn't think badly of him, your Reverence.

THE PASTOR: Afterwards cometh eternal life.

THE DYING MAN: And that'll be better?

THE PASTOR: Yes.

THE DYING MAN: It's got to be.

THE WIFE: He's taken it out of himself, you know.

THE PASTOR: Believe me, God knows it.

THE DYING MAN: You think so? *After a pause*: Up there, I suppose a man'll be able to open his mouth for once now and again?

THE PASTOR *slightly confused*: It is written that faith moveth
  mountains. You must believe. You will find it easier then.

THE WIFE: Your Reverence, you mustn't think he doesn't
  believe. He always took Communion. *To her husband,
  urgently*: Here's his Reverence thinking you don't believe.
  But you do believe, don't you?

THE DYING MAN: Yes . . .

  Silence.

THE DYING MAN: There's nothing else then.

THE PASTOR: What are you trying to say by that? There's
  nothing else then?

THE DYING MAN: Just: there's nothing else then. Eh? I mean,
  suppose there had been anything?

THE PASTOR: But what could there have been?

THE DYING MAN: Anything at all.

THE PASTOR: But you have had your dear wife and your son.

THE WIFE: You had us, didn't you?

THE DYING MAN: Yes . . .

  Silence.

THE DYING MAN: I mean: if life had added up to anything . . .

THE PASTOR: I'm not quite sure I understand you. You surely
  don't mean that you only believe because your life has been
  all toil and hardship?

THE DYING MAN *looks round until he catches sight of his son*:
  And is it going to be better for them?

THE PASTOR: For youth, you mean? Let us hope so.

THE DYING MAN: If the boat had had a motor . . .

THE WIFE: You mustn't worry about that now.

THE PASTOR: It is not a moment to be thinking of such
  things.

THE DYING MAN: I've got to.

THE WIFE: We'll manage all right.

THE DYING MAN: But suppose there's a war?

THE WIFE: Don't speak about that now. *To the pastor*: These
  last times he was always talking to the boy about war. They
  didn't agree about it.

  The pastor looks at the son.

THE SON: He doesn't believe in our future.

THE DYING MAN: Tell me: up there, does *he* want war?

THE PASTOR *hesitating*: It says: Blessed are the peacemakers.

THE DYING MAN: But if there's a war . . .

THE SON: The Führer doesn't want a war!

The dying man makes a wide gesture of the hand, as if shoving that away.

THE DYING MAN: So if there's a war . . .

The son wants to say something.

THE WIFE: Keep quiet now.

THE DYING MAN *to the pastor, pointing at his son*: You tell him that about the peacemakers.

THE PASTOR: We are all in the hand of God, you must not forget.

THE DYING MAN: You telling him?

THE WIFE: But his Reverence can't do anything to stop war, be reasonable. Better not talk about it nowadays, eh, your Reverence?

THE DYING MAN: You know: they're a swindling lot. I can't buy a motor for my boat. Their aeroplanes get motors all right. For war, for killing. And when it's stormy like this I can't bring her in because I haven't a motor. Those swindlers! War's what they're after! *He sinks back exhausted.*

THE WIFE *anxiously fetches a cloth and a bowl of water, and wipes away his sweat*: You mustn't listen. He doesn't know what he's saying.

THE PASTOR: You should calm yourself, Mr Claasen.

THE DYING MAN: You telling him about the peacemakers?

THE PASTOR *after a pause*: He can read for himself. It's in the Sermon on the Mount.

THE DYING MAN: He says it's all written by a Jew and it doesn't apply.

THE WIFE: Don't start on that again! He doesn't mean it like that. That's what he hears the others saying.

THE DYING MAN: Yes. *To the pastor*: Does it apply?

THE WIFE *with an anxious glance at her son*: Don't make trouble for his Reverence, Hannes. You shouldn't ask that.

THE SON: Why shouldn't he ask that?

THE DYING MAN: Does it apply or not?

THE PASTOR: It is also written: Render therefore unto Caesar the things which are Caesar's; and unto God the things that are God's.

The dying man sinks back. His wife lays the damp cloth on his forehead.

21

The motto

> Their boys learn it's morally healthy
> To lay down one's life for the wealthy:
> It's a lesson that's made very clear.
> It's far harder than spelling or figures
> But their teachers are terrible floggers
> So they're fearful of showing fear.

Chemnitz, 1937. Meeting room of the Hitler Youth. A squad of boys, mostly with gasmasks slung round their necks. A small group are looking at a boy with no mask who is sitting by himself on a bench and helplessly moving his lips as if learning something.

THE FIRST BOY: He still hasn't got one.

THE SECOND BOY: His old lady won't buy him one.

THE FIRST BOY: But she must know he'll get into trouble.

THE THIRD BOY: If she ain't got the cash ...

THE FIRST BOY: And old Fatty's got a down on him in any case.

THE SECOND BOY: He's back to learning it: 'The Motto'.

THE FOURTH BOY: That's four weeks he's been trying to learn it, and it's just a couple of verses.

THE THIRD BOY: He's known it off for ages.

THE SECOND BOY: He only gets stuck cause he's frightened.

THE FOURTH BOY: That's terribly funny, don't you think?

THE FIRST BOY: Devastating. *He calls*: D'you know it, Pschierer?

The fifth boy looks up, distracted, gets the meaning and nods. Then he goes on learning.

THE SECOND BOY: Old Fatty only keeps on at him cause he's got no gasmask.

THE THIRD BOY: The way he tells it, it's because he wouldn't go to the pictures with him.

THE FOURTH BOY: That's what I heard too. D'you think it's true?

THE SECOND BOY: Could be, why not? I wouldn't go to the pictures with Fatty either. But he wouldn't start anything with me. My old man wouldn't half kick up a stink.

THE FIRST BOY: Look out, here's Fatty.

The boys come to attention in two ranks. Enter a somewhat corpulent Scharführer. The Hitler salute.

THE SCHARFÜHRER: From the right, number!

They number.

THE SCHARFÜHRER: Gasmasks – on!

The boys put on their gasmasks. Some of them have not got one. They simply go through the motions of the drill.

THE SCHARFÜHRER: We'll start with 'The Motto'. Who's going to recite it for us? *He looks round as if unable to make up his mind, then suddenly*: Pschierer! You do it so nicely.

The fifth boy steps forward and stands to attention in front of the others.

THE SCHARFÜHRER: Can you do it, maestro?

THE FIFTH BOY: Yes, sir!

THE SCHARFÜHRER: Right, get cracking! Verse number one!

THE FIFTH BOY:

Thou shalt gaze on death unblinking –
Saith the motto for our age –
Sent into the fray unflinching
Heedless of the battle's rage.

THE SCHARFÜHRER: Don't wet your pants now. Carry on! Verse number two!

THE FIFTH BOY:

Victory is ours for gaining.
Beat, stab, shoot . . .

He has got stuck, and repeats these words. One or two of the boys find it difficult not to burst out laughing.

THE SCHARFÜHRER: So once again you haven't learnt it?

THE FIFTH BOY: Yes, sir!

THE SCHARFÜHRER: I bet you learn something different at home, don't you? *Shouts:* Carry on!

THE FIFTH BOY:

Beat, stab, shoot them so they fall.
Be a German . . . uncomplaining, uncomplaining
Be a German uncomplaining
Die for this . . . die for this, and give your all.

THE SCHARFÜHRER: Now what's so difficult about that?

22

News of the bombardment of Almería gets to the barracks

The soldiers in His armed forces
Get full meat and pudding courses
And can also ask for more.
It helps them to face the firing
And not to think of enquiring
Who He is fighting for.

Berlin, 1937. Corridor in a barracks. Looking around them nervously, two working-class boys are carrying away something wrapped in brown paper.

THE FIRST BOY: Aren't half worked up today, are they?

THE SECOND BOY: They say it's cause war could break out. Over Spain.

THE FIRST BOY: White as a sheet, some of them.

THE SECOND BOY: Cause we bombarded Almería. Last night.

THE FIRST BOY: Where's that?

THE SECOND BOY: In Spain, silly. Hitler telegraphed for a German warship to bombard Almería right away. As a punishment. Cause they're reds down there, and reds have got to be scared shitless of the Third Reich. Now it could lead to war.

THE FIRST BOY: And now they're scared shitless too.

THE SECOND BOY: Right. Scared shitless, that's them.

THE FIRST BOY: What do they want to go bombarding for if they're white as a sheet and scared shitless cause it could lead to war?

THE SECOND BOY: They just started bombarding cause Hitler wants it that way.

THE FIRST BOY: Whatever Hitler wants they want too. The whole lot are for Hitler. Cause he's built up our new armed forces.

THE SECOND BOY: You got it.

Pause.

THE FIRST BOY: Think we can sneak out now?

THE SECOND BOY: Better wait, or we'll run into one of those lieutenants. Then he'll confiscate everything and they'll be in trouble.

THE FIRST BOY: Decent of them to let us come every day.

THE SECOND BOY: Oh, they ain't millionaires any more than us, you know. They know how it is. My old lady only gets ten marks a week, and there are three of us. It's just enough for potatoes.

THE FIRST BOY: Smashing nosh they get here. Meatballs today.

THE SECOND BOY: How much d'they give you this time?

THE FIRST BOY: One dollop, as usual. Why?

THE SECOND BOY: They gave me two this time.

THE FIRST BOY: Let's see. They only gave one.

The second boy shows him.

THE FIRST BOY: Did you say anything to them?

THE SECOND BOY: No. Just 'good morning' as usual.

THE FIRST BOY: I don't get it. And me too, 'Heil Hitler' as usual.

THE SECOND BOY: Funny. They gave me two dollops.

THE FIRST BOY: Why d'they suddenly do that. I don't get it.

THE SECOND BOY: Nor me. Coast's clear now.

They quickly run off.

23
Job creation

He sees that jobs are provided.
The poor go where they are guided:
He likes them to be keen.
They're allowed to serve the nation.
Their blood and perspiration
Can fuel His war machine.

Spandau, 1937. A worker comes home and finds a neighbour there.

THE NEIGHBOUR: Good evening, Mr Fenn. I just came to see if your wife could lend me some bread. She's popped out for a moment.

THE MAN: That's all right, Mrs Dietz. What d'you think of the job I got?

THE NEIGHBOUR: Ah, they're all getting work. At the new factory, aren't you? You'll be turning out bombers then?

THE MAN: And how.

THE NEIGHBOUR: They'll be needed in Spain these days.

THE MAN: Why specially Spain?

THE NEIGHBOUR: You hear such things about the stuff they're sending. A disgrace, I call it.

THE MAN: Best mind what you say.

THE NEIGHBOUR: You joined them now too?

THE MAN: I've not joined nothing. I get on with my work. Where's Martha gone?

THE NEIGHBOUR: I'd best warn you, I suppose. It could be something nasty. Just as I came in the postman was here, and there was some kind of letter got your wife all worked up. Made me wonder if I shouldn't ask the Schiermanns to lend me that bread.

THE MAN: Cor. *He calls*: Martha!
Enter his wife. She is in mourning.

THE MAN: What are you up to? Who's dead then?

THE WIFE: Franz. We got a letter.
She hands him a letter.

THE NEIGHBOUR: For God's sake! What happened to him?

THE MAN: It was an accident.

THE NEIGHBOUR *mistrustfully*: But wasn't he a pilot?

THE MAN: Yes.

THE NEIGHBOUR: And he had an accident?

THE MAN: At Stettin. In the course of a night exercise with troops, it says here.

THE NEIGHBOUR: He won't have had no accident. Tell me another.

THE MAN: I'm only telling you what it says here. The letter's from the commandant.

THE NEIGHBOUR: Did he write to you lately? From Stettin?

THE MAN: Don't get worked up, Martha. It won't help.

THE WIFE *sobbing*: No, I know.

THE NEIGHBOUR: He was such a nice fellow, that brother of yours. Like me to make you a pot of coffee?

THE MAN: Yes, if you would, Mrs Dietz.

THE NEIGHBOUR *looking for a pot*: That sort of thing's always a shock.

THE WIFE: Go on, have your wash, Herbert. Mrs Dietz won't mind.

THE MAN: There's no hurry.

THE NEIGHBOUR: So he wrote to you from Stettin?

THE MAN: That's where the letters always came from.

THE NEIGHBOUR *gives a look*: Really? I suppose he'd gone south with the others?

THE MAN: What do you mean, gone south?

THE NEIGHBOUR: Way south to sunny Spain.

THE MAN *as his wife again bursts into sobs*: Pull yourself together, Martha. You shouldn't say that sort of thing, Mrs Dietz.

THE NEIGHBOUR: I just wonder what they'd tell you in Stettin if you went and tried to collect your brother.

THE MAN: I'm not going to Stettin.

THE NEIGHBOUR: They always sweep things under the mat. They think it's heroic of them not to let anything come out. There was a fellow in the boozer bragging about how clever they are at covering up their war. When one of your bombers gets shot down and the blokes inside jump out with parachutes, the other bombers machine-gun them down in midair – their own blokes – so's they can't tell the Reds where they've come from.

THE WIFE *who is feeling sick*: Get us some water, will you, Herbert, I'm feeling sick.

THE NEIGHBOUR: I really didn't mean to upset you, it's just the way they cover it all up. They know it's criminal all right and that their war can't stand being exposed. Same in this case. Had an accident in the course of an exercise! What are they exercising at? A war, that's what!

THE MAN: Don't talk so loudly in here, d'you mind? *To his wife*: How are you feeling?

THE NEIGHBOUR: You're another of them keeps quiet about it all. There's your answer, in that letter.

THE MAN: Just shut up, would you?

THE WIFE: Herbert!

THE NEIGHBOUR: So now it's 'shut up, would you?'. Because you got a job. Your brother-in-law got one too, didn't he? Had an 'accident' with one of the same things you're making in that factory.

THE MAN: I don't like that, Mrs Dietz. Me working on 'one of the same things'! What are all the rest of them working on? What's your husband working on? Electric bulbs, isn't it? I suppose they're not for war. Just to give light. But what's the light for? To light tanks, eh? Or a battleship? Or one of those same things? He's only making light bulbs, though. My God, there's nothing left that's not for war. How am I supposed to find a job if I keep telling myself 'not for war!'? D'you want me to starve?

THE NEIGHBOUR *subduedly*: I'm not saying you got to starve. Of course you're right to take the job. I'm just talking about those criminals. A nice kind of job creation, I don't think.

THE MAN *seriously*: And better not go around in black like that, Martha. They don't like it.

THE NEIGHBOUR: The questions it makes people ask: that's what they don't like.

THE WIFE *calmly*: You'd rather I took it off?

THE MAN: Yes, if I'm not to lose my job any minute.

THE WIFE: I'm not taking it off.

THE MAN: What d'you mean?

THE WIFE: I'm not taking it off. My brother's dead. I'm going into mourning.

THE MAN: If you hadn't got it because Rosa bought it when Mother died, you wouldn't be able to go into mourning.

THE WIFE *shouting*: Don't anyone tell me I'm not going into mourning! If they can slaughter him I have a right to cry, don't I? I never heard of such a thing. It's the most inhuman thing ever happened! They're criminals of the lowest kind!

THE NEIGHBOUR *while the man sits speechless with horror*: But Mrs Fenn!

THE MAN *hoarsely*: If you're going to talk like that we could do more than lose our job.

THE WIFE: Let them come and get me, then! They've concentration camps for women too. Let them just put me in one of those because I dare to mind when they kill my brother! What was he in Spain for?

THE MAN: Shut up about Spain!

THE NEIGHBOUR: That kind of talk could get us into trouble, Mrs Fenn.

THE WIFE: Are we to keep quiet just because they might take your job away? Because we'll die of starvation if we don't make bombers for them? And die just the same if we do? Exactly like my Franz? They created a job for him too. Three foot under. He could as well have had that here.

THE MAN *holding a hand over her mouth*: Shut up, will you? It doesn't help.

THE WIFE: What does help then? Do something that does!

24

Consulting the people

> And as the column passes
> We call with urgent voices:
> Can none of you say No?

You've got to make them heed you.
This war to which they lead you
Will soon be your death-blow.

*Berlin. March 13th, 1938. A working-class flat, with two men
and a woman. The constricted space is blocked by a flagpole. A
great noise of jubilation from the radio, with church bells and
the sound of aircraft. A voice is saying 'And now the Führer is
about to enter Vienna.'*

THE WOMAN: It's like the sea.

THE OLDER WORKER: Aye, it's one victory after another for
that fellow.

THE YOUNGER WORKER: And us that gets defeated.

THE WOMAN: That's right.

THE YOUNGER WORKER: Listen to them shouting. Like
they're being given a present.

THE OLDER WORKER: They are. An invasion.

THE YOUNGER WORKER: And then it's what they call
'consulting the people'. 'Ein Volk, ein Reich, ein Führer!'
'A single people, a single empire, a single leader.' 'Willst du
das, Deutscher?' 'You're German, are you in favour?' And
us not able to put out the least little leaflet about this
referendum. Here, in a working-class district like Neukölln.

THE WOMAN: How d'you mean, not able?

THE YOUNGER WORKER: Too dangerous.

THE OLDER WORKER: And just when they've caught Karl.
How are we to get the addresses?

THE YOUNGER WORKER: We'd need someone to do the
writing too.

THE WOMAN *points at the radio*: He had a hundred thousand
men to launch his attack. We need one man. Fine. If he's the
only one who's got what's needed, then he'll score the
victories.

THE YOUNGER WORKER *in anger*: So we can do without Karl.

THE WOMAN: If that's the way you people feel then we may
as well split up.

THE OLDER WORKER: Comrades, there's no use kidding
ourselves. Producing a leaflet's getting harder and harder,
that's a fact. It's no good acting as if we just can't hear all

that victory din – *pointing at the radio. To the woman*: You've got to admit, anyone hearing that sort of thing might think they're getting stronger all the time. It really does sound like a single people, wouldn't you say?

THE WOMAN: It sounds like twenty thousand drunks being stood free beer.

THE YOUNGER WORKER: For all you know we might be the only people to say so.

THE WOMAN: Right. Us and others like us.

The woman smoothes out a small crumpled piece of paper.

THE OLDER WORKER: What have you got there?

THE WOMAN: It's a copy of a letter. There's such a din I can read it out. *She reads*: 'Dear son: Tomorrow I shall have ceased to be. Executions are usually at six a.m. I'm writing now because I want you to know I haven't changed my opinions, nor have I applied for a pardon because I didn't commit any crime. I just served my class. And if it looks as though I got nowhere like that it isn't so. Every man to his post, should be our motto. Our task is very difficult, but it's the greatest one there is – to free the human race from its oppressors. Till that's done life has no other value. Let that out of our sights and the whole human race will relapse into barbarism. You're still quite young but it won't hurt you to remember always which side you are on. Stick with your own class, then your father won't have suffered his unhappy fate in vain, because it isn't easy. Look after your mother, your brothers and sisters too, you're the eldest. Better be clever. Greetings to you all, Your loving Father.'

THE OLDER WORKER: There aren't really that few of us after all.

THE YOUNGER WORKER: What's to go in the referendum leaflet, then?

THE WOMAN *thinking*: Best thing would be just one word: NO!

Additional Texts by Brecht

NOTE TO 'FEAR AND MISERY OF THE THIRD REICH'

The play 'Fear and Misery of the Third Reich' offers the actor more temptation to use an acting method appropriate to a dramaturgically Aristotelian play than do other plays in this collection. To allow it to be performed immediately, under the unfavourable circumstances of exile, it is written in such a way that it can be performed by tiny theatre groups (the existing workers' groups) and in a partial selection (based on a given choice of individual scenes). The workers' groups are neither capable nor desirous of conjuring up the spectators' empathetic feeling: the few professionals at their disposal are versed in the epic method of acting which they learnt from the theatrical experiments of the decade prior to the fascist regime. The acting methods of these professionals accord admirably with those of the workers' groups. Those theorists who have recently taken to treating the *montage* technique as a purely formal principle are hereby confronted with montage as a practical matter, and this may make them shift their speculations back to solid ground.

> [BFA 24, p. 225. Possibly intended for the Malik-Verlag edition. The last sentence is aimed at Georg Lukács, a Hungarian Marxist philosopher and literary critic who rejected literary modernism in favour of a realist approach.]

FURTHER NOTE

The cycle 'Fear and Misery of the Third Reich' is a documentary play. Censorship problems and material difficulties have hitherto prevented the available small workers' theatre groups from performing more than a few isolated scenes. Using simple indications of scenery (for instance, playing against dimly lit swastika flags), however, almost any theatre with a revolving or a multiple set could resolve the play's technical problems. It should be feasible to stage at least a selection of 17 scenes (1, 2, 5, 6, 8, 9, 12, 13, 16, 18, 19, 20, 22, 23, 25, 27). The play shows behaviour patterns typical of people of different classes under Fascist dictatorship, and not only the gests of caution, self-protection, alarm and so forth but also that of resistance need to be brought out. In the series of *Versuche* whose publication began in 1930 this play constitutes no. 20.

[BFA 24, pp. 226–7. May also have been intended for the Malik publication, which was interrupted in 1938/39.]

THE ANXIETIES OF THE REGIME

1
A foreigner, returning from a trip to the Third Reich
When asked who really ruled there, answered:
Fear.

2
Anxiously
The scholar breaks off his discussion to inspect
The thin partitions of his study, his face ashen. The teacher
Lies sleepless, worrying over
An ambiguous phrase the inspector had let fall.
The old woman in the grocer's shop
Puts her trembling finger to her lips to hold back
Her angry exclamation about the bad flour. Anxiously
The doctor inspects the strangulation marks on his patient's throat.
Full of anxiety, parents look at their children as at traitors.
Even the dying

Hush their failing voices as they
Take leave of their relatives.

3
But likewise the brownshirts themselves
Fear the man whose arm doesn't fly up
And are terrified of the man who
Wishes them a good morning.
The shrill voices of those who give orders
Are full of fear like the squeaking of
Piglets awaiting the butcher's knife, as their fat arses
Sweat with anxiety in their office chairs.
Driven by anxiety
They break into homes and search the lavatories
And it is anxiety
That makes them burn whole libraries. Thus
Fear rules not only those who are ruled, but
The rulers too.

4
Why do they so fear the open word?

5
Given the immense power of the regime
Its camps and torture cellars
Its well-fed policemen
Its intimidated or corrupt judges
Its card indexes and lists of suspected persons
Which fill whole buildings to the roof
One would think they wouldn't have to
Fear an open word from a simple man.

6
But their Third Reich recalls
The house of Tar, the Assyrian, that mighty fortress

Which, according to the legend, could not be taken by any army, but
When one single, distinct word was spoken inside it
Fell to dust.

GUNS BEFORE BUTTER

1

The famous remark of General Goering
That guns should come before butter
Is correct inasmuch as the government needs
The more guns the less butter it has
For the less butter it has
The more enemies.

2

Furthermore it should be said that
Guns on an empty stomach
Are not to every people's taste.
Merely swallowing gas
They say, does not quench thirst
And without woollen pants
A soldier, it could be, is brave only in summer.

3

When the artillery runs out of ammunition
Officers up front tend
To get holes in their backs.

[*Poems 1913–1956*, pp. 296–8 and p. 300.]

Notes

Prologue. The German march-past

The opening, free-verse poem of the prologue reflects the tendency within Nazi propaganda to depict Adolf Hitler as a divine figure. The capitalisation of 'He' and the references to 'heavens' portray Hitler as a god-like figure, and anticipate further use of the capitalised pronoun in the opening poems of Scenes 9, 11, 22 and 23. Nevertheless, Hitler's proclaimed Messianic status is immediately questioned in the sceptical phrase: 'He who claimed to have been sent by God'. The following three stanzas, set in the tail-rhyme scheme (aabccb) that predominates throughout the play's verses, introduce the cycle of scenes as a kind of military parade, underlining the militaristic nature of the Third Reich and anticipating the cross-section of society that will soon be parading across the stage. The image of a march-past is nevertheless ironic, since the figures are described as 'a motley sight', some crawling, 'a ramshackle collection'. The expected uniformity of an army is therefore inverted, emphasising the multifarious nature of German society and defiantly refusing to submit to the propagandistic view of the German people as uniformly blond, blue-eyed and committed to the National Socialist cause.

p. 3   *crooked crosses*: swastikas.

Scene 1. One big family
The night of January 30th, 1933
One of only two scenes with specific dates, this scene is set in

Berlin on the night after Hitler has been appointed German Chancellor. Two SS officers, members of Hitler's élite personal guard, appear to be drunk after a day of celebration. Their conversation is littered with Nazi rhetoric, such as the ideals of a united nation and of a moral revival, which Hitler has claimed will be the hallmarks of the Third Reich. Similarly, they set 'German Man' against 'those filthy subhumans', reflecting the Nazi obsession with the ideal German figure and the rejection of all those who do not fit this Aryan mould: principally Jews. Their mention of 'cleaning up a bunch of Marxists' refers to the Communist opponents of the NSDAP in the preceding years, but the implication is that these supposed Marxists were in fact a Catholic youth club. So the indiscriminate nature of Nazi violence and the attacks against the Church later in the 1930s are anticipated. The scene closes as one of the men begins to shoot randomly, terrified when he hears a voice calling from a window. The SS are thus introduced as figures who spread terror that is fuelled by their own fear.

6   *Not one of them was wearing a collar*: no collar on their shirts, i.e. they were workers.

Scene 2. A case of betrayal
Breslau, 1933

In this short scene, a lower-middle-class couple listen as their neighbour is brutally arrested. Although the couple refuse to admit even to themselves that they are responsible for his arrest, the poem at the opening makes their involvement explicit: 'traitors / Who've given away their neighbours'. It is implied that they informed on their neighbour for listening to foreign radio broadcasts. Since the German radio was controlled by the Nazi Party and used principally for propaganda purposes, listening to foreign broadcasts tended to indicate a rejection of the regime. The image of the police as a source of terror rather than protection is evident in the man's refusal to involve himself further in his neighbour's arrest.

6   *Breslau*: the German name for the city of Wroclaw, in present-day Poland. Breslau was part of Germany until 1945.

Scene 3. The chalk cross
Berlin, 1933
This long scene is one of the core scenes, intended by Brecht to form part of any staging of the play. The principal character is an SA man, a member of the paramilitary wing of the NSDAP. He is visiting his girlfriend, a maidservant in a gentleman's house in Berlin, and engages in conversation with the cook, chauffeur and the cook's brother, an unemployed 'worker'. The SA man excitedly narrates his involvement in shock-attacks that spread fear among the population. The fact that he does not give any specific details about who 'the enemy' are, or in which particular parts of Berlin he is active, makes his presence all the more ominous and threatening. The scene is structured by a disturbing interplay between the convivial atmosphere of the colleagues and friends in the kitchen and the sense of impending violence and terror. For example, attention is drawn to the SA man's new boots, which the maidservant describes as 'lovely'. Yet in the context of the man's description of SA activities, these boots evoke physical violence. When the worker enters, he only mumbles the official Nazi greeting, 'Heil Hitler', suggesting that he is not committed to Nazism. The fact that the worker is adept at building radios implies that he listens to foreign broadcasts, since the official state-issued radios could not receive broadcasts from abroad. The worker's apparent dissidence is further compounded by his name, Mr Lincke, which is aurally and visually similar to the German word for 'the left-winger', 'Der Linke'. The 'trick' with the chalk

cross that the SA man shows to the worker emphasises the insidious nature of SA tactics and the danger of speaking one's mind to anybody, even if they appear to encourage such openness. This pervasive distrust is underlined at the end of the scene by the maidservant's realisation that she cannot even trust her boyfriend any more.

7   *brown storm troopers*: 'brownshirts', the SA.

12   *the public welfare*: the office that provides benefits for the unemployed and poor.

13   *that racketeering Republic*: the SA man is referring to the Weimar Republic, Germany's parliamentary democracy from 1919–33. Nazi rhetoric claimed that the Republic was a system of organised extortion ('racketeering'), defrauding the German people of their rightful inheritance.

14   *Our Führer*: 'our leader' – Adolf Hitler.
     Goebbels: Joseph Goebbels (1897–1945) was the Nazi Propaganda Minister from 1933 to 1945.
     voluntary labour service: established in 1931, the Voluntary Labour Service set up programmes to provide work for the unemployed. The term 'voluntary' was somewhat misleading, since the unemployed were often compelled to take work under poor conditions for fear of losing all their benefits, and pay was extremely low. It also served to reduce unemployment figures, but did not improve individuals' standard of living.

15   *Dr Ley*: Robert Ley (1890–1945), head of the German Labour Front (DAF), founded 2 May 1933.
     Strength through Joy: founded in 1933, this organisation aimed to organise the leisure time of the working classes in an attempt to integrate them better into the Third Reich, thus reducing dissatisfaction and dissidence. Typically middle-class activities were extended to workers, such as sailing,

theatre, classical music concerts and holidays to tourist
destinations.

concentration camp: the Nazis established a network of
concentration camps throughout the Reich, the first opening
in 1933. Initially meant to house political prisoners, in the
form of opponents of the regime, they soon began to intern
Jews, Sinti and Roma and homosexuals.

Baron Thyssen: Fritz Thyssen (1878–1951) was a German
industrialist and steel magnate who contributed funds to the
Nazi Party in the early 1930s and strongly supported Hitler's
bid for the chancellorship in 1932–3. The worker makes
ironic mention of him, implying that the NSDAP
membership of a wealthy aristocrat goes against the Nazis'
claims of eradicating class divides.

16   *From fifty pfennigs to one mark*: according to the worker's
story, the price of margarine has doubled under Hitler.

Winter Aid: a Nazi organisation funded by donations from
German citizens to provide clothing, food and money for
those in need.

Goering: Hermann Goering (1893–1946) was commander of
the Luftwaffe (the German Air Force) and second-in-
command of the Third Reich.

21   *Mein Kampf*: Hitler wrote this book ('My Struggle') detailing
his political vision while he was interned in Landsberg in the
mid-1920s.

Scene 4. Peat-bog soldiers
Esterwegen concentration camp, 1934
This scene is set in a concentration camp for political prisoners in
Esterwegen, in the Emsland region of north-western Germany. The
characters, here mixing cement, represent a cross-section of the
kinds of people who were interned by the Nazis in the early years

of the Third Reich: Communists, Social Democrats, Jehovah's Witnesses. Dievenbach, who claims to be apolitical, accuses both Brühl (a Social Democrat) and Lohmann (a Communist) of being responsible for Hitler's rise to power, since they failed to form a 'united front' against the NSDAP (for if the Socialists and Communists had joined forces in the November 1932 election, they would have defeated the NSDAP). Lohmann and Brühl, in turn, accuse each other's parties of responsibility for the current state of affairs, and almost come to blows. Yet when the SS guard demands to know who cried out 'Traitors', they all remain silent in order to protect one another, and consequently are all given solitary confinement. So the 'united front' is ultimately created in the concentration camp, through the prisoners' fear of the SS.

22   *storm troopers*: members of the SS.

Lenin and Kautsky: Vladimir Lenin (1870–1924) was the first leader of the Soviet Union and as such stands here for Soviet Communism, represented in the scene by Brühl. Karl Kautsky (1854–1938) was a leading theoretician of social democracy and a detractor of Communism, and so represents Lohmann's position in this scene.

23   '*Song of the Peat-bog Soldiers*': this song is one of the most well-known protest songs of twentieth-century Europe. It originated in the concentration camps in Emsland during the 1930s and expresses the prisoners' lament at the harsh conditions under which they labour as well as their hope for future liberation.

Reichstag: the German parliament.

Scene 5. Servants of the people
Oranienburg concentration camp, 1934
This short scene takes place in a concentration camp near Berlin. A detainee is being flogged by an SS guard, who appears to see this

brutal act as merely a tiring and irritating part of his job. His indifference to the task is reflected in the fact that, on the detainee's request, he does not whip his stomach (one of the most sensitive parts of the body). By contrast, his superior officer's cruelty is demonstrated by him ordering the guard to whip the stomach. This blatant contempt for human life is reflected in the opening poem, in the ironic reference to the camp warders as 'the people's servants'. This scene also goes some way to commenting on the hierarchical structure of the Nazi apparatus of terror, such that the lower echelons – here an SS guard – who actually carry out the violent treatment are following orders from their superiors. Further, the shadowy figure of Klapproth, who apparently enjoys flogging, introduces the image of sadistic guards who take pleasure in carrying out these orders.

Scene 6. Judicial process
Augsburg, 1934
Set in Brecht's home town of Augsburg in southern Germany, this is another of his core scenes. The idea of service to the people is thematised once again in the opening poem, this time in the suggestion that 'justice' is no longer an objective notion, but is 'what serves our People best'. The difficulty of interpreting such a directive is articulated in the poem, and the rhyming of 'What serves our people best' with 'The whole people is under arrest' succinctly anticipates the police state that the Third Reich was to become. The scene itself then illustrates the strains and failure of the justice system. The main character is a judge who is forced to base his judgement on a particular case not on an impartial examination of the evidence, but on considerations of how a particular judgement would be viewed by the SA and the Ministry of Justice. His decision is therefore influenced substantially by fears for his own career and even his own safety and that of his family.

All of these complex machinations are thrown into relief by a brief interlude with the judge's maidservant, a genuinely caring figure who appears to be the only one to speak honestly in stating that the SA are mainly former criminals and are terrorising the neighbourhood. She clearly expects the judge to find the SA men guilty of the attack and theft, but the impossibility of the judge being able to do so is emphasised by the crowds cramming into the courtroom, including many SA men. In a final twist, the judge picks up his address book instead of the case file, making plain the fact that his judgement is to be based not on the evidence collected but on the relationships between those involved and between himself, the SA and the Ministry of Justice.

28   *racial profanation*: a Nazi term for sexual relations between a Jew and an Aryan. In the course of the scene it becomes evident that these relations were conducted between Arndt's daughter and an SA man, and that the SA therefore do not wish it to become public knowledge.

31   *the Silesian backwoods*: the prosecutor suggests that if the judge does not discharge his duties satisfactorily, he may be transferred to a rural area in the far eastern corner of the Reich. The reference to being moved east, and the comment that 'it's not all that cosy there these days' introduces undertones of deportation to Nazi concentration camps.

34   *Justice is what serves the German people best*: the prosecutor is quoting the Reich Commissioner for Justice, Hans Frank: 'Recht ist, was dem deutschen Volke nützt, Unrecht, was ihm schadet.'

35   *Pontius Pilate and the Creed*: the Creed (the Christian statement of belief) declares that Jesus Christ 'suffered under Pontius Pilate', the governor of Judea, who reluctantly ordered Christ's crucifixion although he was not convinced that Christ was guilty of conspiring against Rome.

Scene 7. Occupational disease
Berlin, 1934

In this scene, the field of medicine in the Third Reich is placed under the microscope. A surgeon takes a group of assistants around the ward, impressing upon them the prevalence of occupational diseases and the consequent necessity of asking questions about the patients' backgrounds. The fact that the surgeon fails to ask questions when he is confronted with a patient covered in open wounds, supposedly caused by falling down some stairs, highlights the hypocrisy of the profession under the Nazi regime. It takes two of the assistants to answer the questions that the surgeon should have been asking: that the patient is a worker interned in the concentration camp in Oranienburg, near Berlin, and that this is therefore also a case of 'occupational disease'. The implication is thus that being a member of the working classes was enough to bring about imprisonment and torture.

Scene 8. The physicists
Göttingen, 1935

A prominent university city, Göttingen is the setting for this scene portraying the negative impact of the Nazi regime on scientific research. Two physicists, their fear at being discovered reflected in their naming as 'X' and 'Y', are discussing Y's correspondence with Albert Einstein. The famous Jewish-German physicist and Nobel Prize-winner, who emigrated to the United States in 1933 in order to avoid Nazi persecution, has written to them with answers to some queries relating to their work on the Theory of Relativity. The extreme danger of corresponding with Einstein, for which physicists could be blacklisted or worse, is palpable in the extreme caution that they exercise when discussing Einstein's ideas, for fear of being overheard. Nazism's detrimental effect on scientific inquiry is thereby brought to the fore.

44   *Newtons*: Sir Isaac Newton 1643–1727, an English physicist.

Scene 9. The Jewish wife
Frankfurt, 1935
In another of Brecht's core scenes, the playwright tackles the issue of marriages between Jews and non-Jews in the Third Reich. The date is significant here, since 1935 was the year in which the Nuremberg Race Laws were pronounced, according to which such 'mixed' marriages were prohibited. Rather than portray a couple who are unable to marry as a result, Brecht approaches the topic from a less obvious angle, presenting a Jewish wife and a non-Jewish husband. The premise is that the husband's profession as doctor is being put at risk by his wife's status as a Jew, and she has decided to flee to Amsterdam in the Netherlands in order to remove this impediment to his career. Most of the scene is a monologue, and is by far the most moving of the play, as the wife makes telephone calls to arrange for her husband to be looked after by friends and family while she is away, and then rehearses ways in which she might break the news to her husband. The way in which the Third Reich stymies free speech even among close friends and family is made plain here, as both husband and wife pretend that she will return in a matter of weeks, while at the same time packing her winter coat – which she will not need for months.

50   *quantum theory and the Trendelenburg test*: in a nod to the two previous scenes, the wife laments the absurdity of life in Germany: that the same people who were enlightened enough to make such huge scientific advances have allowed themselves to be oppressed by 'a lot of semi-barbarians' and so to lose control even over their personal relationships. Quantum theory is a significant part of Einstein's work, and therefore alludes to Scene 8. The Trendelenburg test is a test

for varicose veins, named after a German surgeon who
trained at the Charité hospital in Berlin, and so recalls
Scene 7.

51   *I'll see they give me a special permit*: the husband is
probably referring to the restrictions placed on what one was
allowed to post in the Third Reich. He will attempt to gain a
special permit to send more money than would otherwise be
allowed.

Scene 10. The spy
Cologne, 1935

This final core scene takes place on a Sunday afternoon, in the
home of a married couple with a ten-year-old son, Klaus-Heinrich.
The father is a teacher. As the scene opens, the father refuses to
take a call from one of his colleagues, Mr Klimbtsch. The
implication is that the father is ignoring this colleague because he is
unpopular with the school authorities, and therefore that any
association could reflect badly on him. Instead, they seem to have
more time for the Lemkes, who are evidently more loyal to the
Nazi regime. The father makes derogatory comments about the
regime, but has to bite his tongue in front of their maidservant,
since her father is the 'block warden'. These wardens are low-
ranking Nazi officials responsible for the political supervision of
their neighbourhood, which included passing on information to
higher authorities about potentially dissident citizens. The parents
suddenly notice that Klaus-Heinrich has disappeared, and become
worried that he is informing the Hitler Youth leaders of his
father's criticisms of the Nazi regime. The Hitler Youth, founded
in 1926, was the male youth wing of the Nazi Party, for boys aged
fourteen and above. Its members were encouraged by the leaders to
inform on any subversive behaviour or discussion, including by
their own parents. Even when Klaus-Heinrich returns, and insists

that he simply went out to buy some sweets, the parents feel
unable to trust him.

52   *The Youth Movement*: the youth apparatus of the Nazi
      Party, including the Hitler Youth and the League of German
      Girls.
      Himmler: Heinrich Himmler (1900–45) was head of the SS
      and of the German police, and overseer of the Nazi
      concentration and extermination camps.

54   *group leader*: the boy is referring to the leader of his Hitler
      Youth group.
      cases against priests: in 1935, there was a huge increase in the
      amount of trials against Catholic priests accused of sex
      crimes (especially homosexuality), part of the Nazi Party's
      attempts to reduce the power of the Church.

55   *that Brown House*: the headquarters of the Nazi Party, in
      Munich, was called the 'Brown House'.

60   *taking the socialist paper* [. . .] *hanging out the old nationalist
      flag*: subscription to a socialist newspaper would have made
      their neighbours, the Gauffs, objects of suspicion in the
      Third Reich. The flag is the black/white/red symbol of the
      former German Empire (1871–1918). Hanging that flag in
      1933 instead of the swastika implied rejection of the Nazi
      regime.

61   *Bismarck*: Otto von Bismarck (1815–98) was the politician
      who oversaw the unification of Germany in 1871, and served
      as the Empire's first Chancellor.

Scene 11. The black shoes
Bitterfeld, 1935

Like the previous scene, this one addresses the issue of the Nazi
Youth Movement. In addition, it thematises the poverty that was
still prevalent in many German cities, despite Hitler's claims to the

contrary. Here, the mother cannot afford meat for her growing daughter, and has to take clothing from the welfare office. Despite this dire financial state, she is still under pressure to pay for her daughter to attend the Hitler Youth. The daughter's references to town and country getting to know one another are an allusion to Hitler's policy of integration between rural and urban areas. One section of the Nazi Youth Movement was the 'countryside service' (Landdienst), which sent young people from the cities to visit and work on farms. This policy was based on Hitler's 'Blood and Soil' ideology, namely that a pure German race was based on descent and homeland, and therefore that the rural dwellers represented the purest Germans.

Scene 12. Labour service
The Lüneberger Heide, 1935

This scene portrays two workers in the Nazi Labour Service. From 1935 onwards, all young men were obliged to do six months' labour, under the remit of the German army. As the scene suggests, it was supposedly an attempt to remove class barriers by bringing the lower classes and the bourgeoisie (here represented by the student) together. However, the mention in the opening line of one worker's imprisonment ('in clink'), apparently for speaking out of line, suggests that this Labour Service is just as repressive as the concentration camps that have been represented in earlier scenes. Furthermore, the student is evidently paying the young worker in cigarettes for doing his share of the work. Class barriers, then, are upheld.

Scene 13. Workers' playtime
Leipzig, 1934

A broadcast for the radio is being produced about working

conditions in a factory. The intention to use it as propaganda is expressed by the reference to Goebbels, the Nazi Propaganda Minister. The announcer attempts to articulate the party line – that workers are co-operating happily to provide for the German population. However, the workers whom he interviews are less than enthusiastic, and so the announcer is forced to adjust all their utterances in order to follow that party line, effectively putting words into the workers' mouths. In this context, the announcer makes several references to 'that rotten old Weimar Republic', attempting to portray the Third Reich positively in comparison to the parliamentary democracy that preceded it. However, these attempts are constantly foiled by the morose comments of the workers, whose honest remarks about the working conditions paint the Third Reich in a much less favourable light. The silent presence of an SA man implies that the workers will be punished if they do not toe the party line for this broadcast.

Scene 14. The box
Essen, 1934

In a working-class flat, a woman receives her husband's body from the SA, who claim that he died of pneumonia. However, it is evident that he was murdered by the SA for speaking out against the Nazi regime by claiming that he was receiving 'starvation wages', i.e. too little to live on. The reference to the daughter's lung trouble and to their inability to afford milk emphasises this poverty and sets up links to other scenes in which the deprivation of the working classes is thematised. The SA have sealed the husband in a zinc coffin, to prevent his family opening it and seeing his tortured body. While the worker wants to open the coffin and see the body, the woman is more realistic, aware that doing so would endanger those involved and their families. Again, the fear of both persecutor and persecuted comes to the fore: the

SA are frightened that their murder will be uncovered; and the woman refuses to speak the truth for fear of reprisals.

Scene 15. Release
Berlin, 1936
This scene portrays the return home of a concentration camp inmate. It appears that he was interned for dissident activity, and it is implied that his neighbours, whom he visits in the scene, are also sympathetic to the cause. Moreover, the allusions to his wife, Selma, being 'laid up' indicate that she also suffered violence at the hands of those who arrested her husband. The neighbours are fearful that the released man has given in to the torture to which he has been subjected in the camp, and become an informer, and therefore they resolve not to betray themselves to him. The scene gradually increases in tension as the conversation moves from the safe topics of small talk to more delicate matters: Selma's injuries, gentle gibes at the lack of press freedom, the released man's mangled hand (presumably the result of torture). Finally, the released man attempts to reassure the distrustful couple by claiming that he has not changed, but even then his neighbour feels unable to trust him fully. Since the three of them leave together at the end of the scene, ostensibly to go for a stroll, this sense of common purpose implies that their resistance will continue. Nevertheless, Brecht himself stated that the doubt as to whether the released man is to be trusted should remain ambiguous in this scene.[1] The friends speak a clipped, colloquial German, reflecting their class as well as the urgency and furtiveness of their situation – an example of the wide range of registers Brecht employs in this play, something which is not so obvious in translation.

70   *Siemens*: a large engineering company that supported the

[1]Letter to Wieland Herzfelde, 7 June 1938, *BFA* 29, pp. 98–9.

Nazi Party, manufactured military implements and electronics and used slave labour drawn from the Nazi concentration camps.

71   *You could land up in Bavaria*: the released man seems to know several inmates of concentration camps, suggesting that he is part of a wide resistance network. Bavaria is in southern Germany, while Berlin is in the north. The allusion may be to Dachau, the Nazi's first concentration camp, near Munich in Bavaria.

Völkischer Beobachter: the daily newspaper of the NSDAP from 1923 onwards, essentially a propaganda vehicle full of anti-Jewish and pro-Nazi articles. The friends are implying that all newspapers are as propagandistic as the *Völkischer Beobachter*.

Scene 16. Charity begins at home
Karlsruhe, 1937

An old woman receives a parcel from the Winter Aid Organisation, a Nazi organisation funded by donations from German citizens to provide clothing, food and money for those in need. It was under the remit of the Propaganda Ministry, and indeed the fact that the parcel is described as 'a present from the Führer' emphasises the aim of improving Hitler's and the NSDAP's image among German citizens. The parcel is delivered by SA men, who are usually associated with violence and oppression, and by the end of the short scene they have reverted to type, arresting the daughter for supposedly subversive activities. The old woman has inadvertently disclosed that her daughter and son-in-law have been complaining about the rising food prices.

74   *Heil Hitler*: this Nazi greeting became the official greeting in Germany as of 1933. To fail to say it, or to say it

half-heartedly, could be interpreted as an act of rebellion against the regime.

74   *Nice nest of Marxists we've stumbled on here*: the SA men accuse the woman of being a Communist, and therefore an opponent of Hitler's regime. The German Communist Party (KPD) was banned in February 1933.

Scene 17. Two bakers
Landsberg, 1936
This very short scene is structured like an anecdotal joke, emphasising the absurdity of the Nazi regime. Two bakers are both in prison, the first was imprisoned two years ago for mixing bran in with his bread. The second has just been interned for refusing to mix bran and potatoes in his bread. This pithy story thus expresses the hypocrisy of the Nazi law-makers and the difficulty for normal workers of staying on the right side of the law. Their conversation is punctuated with cries of 'Look out!', reflecting the danger of speaking openly about such matters. A further irony is brought out by the location: Landsberg prison is where Hitler was interned in 1924, after his failed Beerhall putsch. So the bakers' stories, demonstrating how the world has been turned on its head, reflect the greater absurdity of Hitler's progression from imprisoned to imprisoner.

Scene 18. The farmer feeds his sow
Aichach, 1937
In September 1936, a series of economic reforms were introduced, known as the Four-Year Plan. This scene displays the consequences of such measures on the ground, for farmers and their crops and animals. The farmer has been ordered by the government to deliver all his grain to the state, rather than using any of it to feed his

animals. Yet he cannot afford the overpriced animal feed that the state is offering for purchase, and so has no option but either to let his pig die or to go against the state's orders. The fact that the Four-Year Plan was aimed more at rearmament, in preparation for the impending war, than at providing for German citizens, is implied by the farmer's complaint that these measures are to help 'that spiv' (Hitler) buy guns. Two further new themes are introduced by the farmer's wife in this scene: the latent anti-Jewish sentiment of ordinary Germans; and the subtle resistance of the clergy. The wife's complaint, 'They got the Jews out but the State's the worst Jew of them all', does not suggest any rejection of the Nazi Party's anti-Jewish policies, but is the wife's way of complaining about the State's acquisitive and avaricious nature, characteristics associated with Jews according to anti-Semitic prejudice.

Scene 19. The old militant
Calw (Württemberg), 1938

The scene takes place in a small town in southern Germany, described generically in the stage directions and therefore standing for any such town in Germany at this time. The lack of foodstuffs such as butter, cream and meat underlies the whole scene. The 'petit-bourgeois' character is the first figure from this social stratum to appear in the play. His detached comments about the need for 'foresight' suggest that his class have not been so badly affected by the food shortages as the working classes have been, yet his horror when it is suggested that the Nazis may begin cancelling mortgages indicates that those of his class may yet be damaged financially by the regime. 'Old militant' was the term used during the Third Reich for those who had joined the NSDAP before 1930. They were therefore originally committed to Hitler's cause and yet often disappointed by the way in which the Third Reich developed. This scene portrays one such figure, in the form of the butcher, who has been a member of the Nazi Party since 1929 and who was a zealous Nazi before he became frustrated by the shortages, deception and coercion that define his experience of the Third Reich. His enthusiasm has now been taken over by the young fellow in the scene. Representative of a typical young Nazi follower, he is excited by the Party's militancy and territorial gains, while the butcher's commitment had ensued from a belief in the anti-individualistic philosophy of Nazism in the 1920s.

77   *Germany needs guns, not butter*: the young fellow is referring to Hermann Goering's statement in 1936 that Germany needed guns instead of butter. Reich Marshall Goering (1893–1946) was second in command to Hitler, and in charge of the Four-Year Plan. Cf. Brecht's poem 'Guns before butter' (see Additional Texts).

    reoccupied the Rhineland: Germany had been forced to cede the territory around the Rhine river after the First World War. By reoccupying it in 1936, Hitler violated the terms of the Treaty of Versailles and asserted Germany's defiance of foreign interference.

Scene 20. The Sermon on the Mount
Lübeck, 1937
A fisherman lies dying, with his wife, son and the pastor by his bedside. The son is dressed in SA uniform and barely speaks, a shadowy figure who nevertheless influences much of the conversation through his presence. The fisherman is distressed at the deception, lack of free speech and war-mongering of the Third Reich, and has evidently been arguing about this with his son. The fisherman is convinced that the country is re-arming, and this is

why he has been unable to source a motor for his fishing boat, which has caused him great difficulty in stormy weather. The son represents the short-sighted nature of many Nazi followers, repeating Hitler's line that he does not want to go to war, and refusing to accept the evidence to the contrary. The Sermon on the Mount is a speech given by Jesus that summarises his principal teachings, as reported in the Gospel of Matthew in the New Testament. It includes the saying 'Blessed are the peacemakers; for they shall be called the children of God' (Matthew 5: 9). The fisherman calls on this blessing as a protest against the Nazi war-mongers. However, the pastor refuses to acknowledge this biblical reference, for fear that he will be reported to the SA by the man's son. Instead, the passage of scripture that he cites (Matthew 22: 21) makes a clear distinction between Caesar (here representing Hitler as Head of State) and God, and therefore implies that the Church should not interfere with the workings of the state. The extent of this anti-Christian sentiment is summarised in the opening poem, in which the Nazi persecution of the Church ('Her broken head is bleeding') and the idolatry of Nazism ('For new gods are succeeding') are expressed.

Scene 21. The motto
Chemnitz, 1937

This scene takes the audience into a Hitler Youth meeting room. A group of boys are discussing a boy who is sitting on his own, and is one of the only ones without a gasmask. The fact that his mother refuses to buy him one implies that the family are not loyal to Hitler, compounded by the Scharführer's comment: 'I bet you learn something different at home, don't you?' He is called on to recite the Hitler Youth 'Motto', but is too terrified to remember it properly. His fearful, stuttering recitation makes the sinister nature of the words all the more patent, with their emphasis on militancy and self-sacrifice. The Scharführer's final question, 'Now what's so difficult about that?' provides the scene with an ironic twist, since it can refer both to reciting the motto and to dying for one's country. Further, the moral improvement that was supposedly the aim of the Hitler Youth is questioned by the implication that the Group Leader makes sexual advances towards the boys.

84   *The Hitler salute*: the official salute of the Third Reich: standing to attention with one's right arm held out straight, pointing upwards.

Scene 22. News of the bombardment of Almería gets to the barracks
Berlin, 1937

Two working-class boys are leaving the army barracks, having collected their daily helping of food. The soldiers, aware of the destitution of working-class families, give these boys some extra food every day. The boys have perceived a heightened sense of fear in the barracks, which they attribute to the fact that Hitler's forces have just bombed the city of Almería in southern Spain, making war seem all the more likely. The 'reds' to whom the boys refer are the Spanish Republicans, left-wing forces who are engaged in a civil war against the Nationalist forces under General Franco. German forces shelled Almería in May 1937, in support of Franco's troops. The boys' perceptive observation is that fear breeds fear: the 'reds' are terrified of the Third Reich, and consequently the German forces are terrified of them. A subtle form of resistance is evident in the fact that the German soldiers give a double portion to the boy who does *not* greet them with 'Heil Hitler'.

Scene 23. Job creation
Spandau, 1937

The conflict in Spain also takes centre-stage in this scene. In Spandau, near Berlin, a woman has just received word that her brother, a pilot, has died. Although she is told that he died during a night exercise in Stettin, north-east of Berlin, her neighbour insists that he must have been involved in the fighting in Spain. The neighbour appears to enjoy the secretive gossip, accusing the Nazi administration of covering up the war, calling them criminals, and accusing the woman's husband of complicity because he works in a munitions factory. However, when the woman takes over the neighbour's anti-Nazi mantra, her husband and the neighbour warn her about the risks of such open condemnation. The neighbour's tendency to meddle and her disingenuous treatment of the couple lead the audience to suspect that she might even turn her neighbours in to the authorities.

Scene 24. Consulting the people
Berlin, March 13th, 1938

The scene is set in a flat in Neukölln, a working-class district of Berlin. A group of workers who produce anti-Nazi leaflets are listening to a radio broadcast of Hitler entering Vienna following the annexation of Austria. The scene's title, 'Consulting the people', refers to the referendum held in April 1938, according to which ninety-nine per cent of the population were in favour of the annexation. The workers are all but ready to give up their resistance, since their position has become so dangerous and defeat seems inevitable, but are spurred on by a letter from a condemned resistance fighter to his young son, encouraging him always to fight oppression. This gives the workers hope, through the sense that they are not alone in their struggle, and so they resolve to produce a leaflet against the referendum.

Questions for Further Study

1   What problems in terms of casting and stage design does the play pose? How would you address these problems if you were producing the play?

2   Consider how you would cast the play. For instance, would you cast the same actors as the Nazi characters in each scene? Explain your decisions.

3   How would you direct the actors to ensure, where appropriate, that the comedy in the play is brought out?

4   Consider how sound, lighting, set and costume design might be used to create an appropriate atmosphere for the play.

5   Fear and misery are central themes in the play. How might these states be expressed on stage through movement, make-up and set design?

6   How would you wish your audience to respond to the Nazi characters in the play? Does this vary from scene to scene? How would you direct the actors to bring out these effects?

7   How might you direct the Jewish wife character, to create a tension in the scene between alienation and empathy?

8   The commentary gives two examples of how the scenes were framed for a production. In what other ways might the existing text be adapted for performance?

9   What theatrical techniques could be used in order to explain the context of the play to a twenty-first-century audience?

10 Brecht nominated four scenes as the play's core scenes, to be included in every production: 'The chalk cross', 'Judicial process', 'The Jewish wife' and 'The spy'. Why do you think

that he selected these particular scenes? Can you make a case for the inclusion of other scenes as core scenes?

11   Which scenes would you choose to present in order to make a coherent production?

12   As a director, how would you present the poems that open each scene, in order to achieve your preferred effects for an audience?

13   How might the play be updated for a production in the twenty-first century?

14   Brecht insisted that the play is 'a piece of epic theatre'. How can this claim be justified?

15   What is the relationship between the realistic and the epic in the play?

16   Would it be possible to stage the play in a completely non-Brechtian (Stanislavskian) mode? If so, what effects might this have on an audience?

17   Some of the play's characters are named, but others are known solely by their position or profession. How does this affect the audience's response to the characters?

18   Are the audience encouraged to empathise with or pity any of the characters? If so, how is this effect achieved?

19   In what ways is the play a political satire? Which scenes are particularly satirical, and why?

20   Is the play only relevant to the specific period of the Third Reich, or does it resonate beyond that particular place and time?

21   Is detailed historical knowledge of this period in Germany necessary in order to understand and appreciate the play?

22   What features of the Third Reich does Brecht depict in the play? How does this depiction compare with other images of Hitler's Germany that you have encountered?

23   Is the play of use as a historical document?

24   What is the relationship between the Christian religion and

the Third Reich in the play? Is this a fair treatment of that relationship?

25 Critics have often attacked the play for failing to portray a positive model of resistance. How would you defend the play against this criticism? How does it reflect the real nature of resistance movements in the Third Reich?

26 How are the working classes represented in the play? What is the relationship between the working classes and resistance?

27 Brecht was a committed Communist. Explain how you understand this term and how this commitment is evident in the play itself.

28 Brecht insisted that the play represented a cross-section of all classes and ranks of German society. To what extent is this true?

CHARLOTTE RYLAND studied at Selwyn College, Cambridge, St John's College, Oxford, and University College London, where she completed a doctorate on the German-language poet Paul Celan. She has taught German at UCL and Oxford University, and her research interests are in twentieth-century German literature, with a particular focus on the impact of the Holocaust.

Methuen Drama Student Editions

Jean Anouilh *Antigone* • John Arden *Serjeant Musgrave's Dance*
Alan Ayckbourn *Confusions* • Aphra Behn *The Rover*
Edward Bond *Lear* • *Saved* • Bertolt Brecht *The Caucasian Chalk Circle*
Fear and Misery in the Third Reich • *The Good Person of Szechwan*
Life of Galileo • *Mother Courage and her Children*
The Resistible Rise of Arturo Ui • *The Threepenny Opera*
Anton Chekhov *The Cherry Orchard* • *The Seagull* • *Three Sisters*
Uncle Vanya • Caryl Churchill *Serious Money* • *Top Girls*
Shelagh Delaney *A Taste of Honey* • Euripides *Elektra* • *Medea*
Dario Fo *Accidental Death of an Anarchist* • Michael Frayn *Copenhagen*
John Galsworthy *Strife* • Nikolai Gogol *The Government Inspector*
Robert Holman *Across Oka* • Henrik Ibsen *A Doll's House* • *Ghosts*
Hedda Gabler • Charlotte Keatley *My Mother Said I Never Should*
Bernard Kops *Dreams of Anne Frank* • Federico García Lorca
Blood Wedding • *Doña Rosita the Spinster* (bilingual edition) • *The House*
of Bernarda Alba • (bilingual edition) • *Yerma* (bilingual edition)
David Mamet *Glengarry Glen Ross* • *Oleanna* • Patrick Marber
Closer • John Marston *Malcontent* • Martin McDonagh *The Lieutenant*
of Inishmore • Joe Orton *Loot* • Luigi Pirandello *Six Characters in Search*
of an Author • Mark Ravenhill *Shopping and F***ing* • Willy Russell
Blood Brothers • *Educating Rita* • Sophocles *Antigone* • *Oedipus the*
King • Wole Soyinka *Death and the King's Horseman* • Shelagh
Stephenson *The Memory of Water* • August Strindberg *Miss Julie*
J. M. Synge *The Playboy of the Western World* • Theatre Workshop *Oh*
What a Lovely War • Timberlake Wertenbaker *Our Country's Good*
Arnold Wesker *The Merchant* • Oscar Wilde *The Importance of Being*
Earnest • Tennessee Williams *A Streetcar Named Desire*
The Glass Menagerie

Methuen Drama Modern Plays

include work by

Edward Albee
Jean Anouilh
John Arden
Margaretta D'Arcy
Peter Barnes
Sebastian Barry
Brendan Behan
Dermot Bolger
Edward Bond
Bertolt Brecht
Howard Brenton
Anthony Burgess
Simon Burke
Jim Cartwright
Caryl Churchill
Complicite
Noël Coward
Lucinda Coxon
Sarah Daniels
Nick Darke
Nick Dear
Shelagh Delaney
David Edgar
David Eldridge
Dario Fo
Michael Frayn
John Godber
Paul Godfrey
David Greig
John Guare
Peter Handke
David Harrower
Jonathan Harvey
Iain Heggie
Declan Hughes
Terry Johnson
Sarah Kane
Charlotte Keatley
Barrie Keeffe

Howard Korder
Robert Lepage
Doug Lucie
Martin McDonagh
John McGrath
Terrence McNally
David Mamet
Patrick Marber
Arthur Miller
Mtwa, Ngema & Simon
Tom Murphy
Phyllis Nagy
Peter Nichols
Sean O'Brien
Joseph O'Connor
Joe Orton
Louise Page
Joe Penhall
Luigi Pirandello
Stephen Poliakoff
Franca Rame
Mark Ravenhill
Philip Ridley
Reginald Rose
Willy Russell
Jean-Paul Sartre
Sam Shepard
Wole Soyinka
Simon Stephens
Shelagh Stephenson
Peter Straughan
C. P. Taylor
Theatre Workshop
Sue Townsend
Judy Upton
Timberlake Wertenbaker
Roy Williams
Snoo Wilson
Victoria Wood

Methuen Drama Contemporary Dramatists

include

John Arden (two volumes)
Arden & D'Arcy
Peter Barnes (three volumes)
Sebastian Barry
Dermot Bolger
Edward Bond (eight volumes)
Howard Brenton
 (two volumes)
Richard Cameron
Jim Cartwright
Caryl Churchill (two volumes)
Sarah Daniels (two volumes)
Nick Darke
David Edgar (three volumes)
David Eldridge
Ben Elton
Dario Fo (two volumes)
Michael Frayn (three volumes)
John Godber (four volumes)
Paul Godfrey
David Greig
John Guare
Lee Hall (two volumes)
Peter Handke
Jonathan Harvey
 (two volumes)
Declan Hughes
Terry Johnson (three volumes)
Sarah Kane
Barrie Keeffe
Bernard-Marie Koltès
 (two volumes)
Franz Xaver Kroetz
David Lan
Bryony Lavery
Deborah Levy
Doug Lucie

David Mamet (four volumes)
Martin McDonagh
Duncan McLean
Anthony Minghella
 (two volumes)
Tom Murphy (five volumes)
Phyllis Nagy
Anthony Neilson (two volumes)
Philip Osment
Gary Owen
Louise Page
Stewart Parker (two volumes)
Joe Penhall (two volumes)
Stephen Poliakoff
 (three volumes)
David Rabe (two volumes)
Mark Ravenhill (two volumes)
Christina Reid
Philip Ridley
Willy Russell
Eric-Emmanuel Schmitt
Ntozake Shange
Sam Shepard (two volumes)
Wole Soyinka (two volumes)
Simon Stephens (two volumes)
Shelagh Stephenson
David Storey (three volumes)
Sue Townsend
Judy Upton
Michel Vinaver
 (two volumes)
Arnold Wesker (two volumes)
Michael Wilcox
Roy Williams (three volumes)
Snoo Wilson (two volumes)
David Wood (two volumes)
Victoria Wood

Methuen Drama World Classics

include

Jean Anouilh (two volumes)
Brendan Behan
Aphra Behn
Bertolt Brecht (eight volumes)
Büchner
Bulgakov
Calderón
Čapek
Anton Chekhov
Noël Coward (eight volumes)
Feydeau
Eduardo De Filippo
Max Frisch
John Galsworthy
Gogol
Gorky (two volumes)
Harley Granville Barker
  (two volumes)
Victor Hugo
Henrik Ibsen (six volumes)
Jarry

Lorca (three volumes)
Marivaux
Mustapha Matura
David Mercer (two volumes)
Arthur Miller (five volumes)
Molière
Musset
Peter Nichols (two volumes)
Joe Orton
A. W. Pinero
Luigi Pirandello
Terence Rattigan
  (two volumes)
W. Somerset Maugham
  (two volumes)
August Strindberg
  (three volumes)
J. M. Synge
Ramón del Valle-Inclán
Frank Wedekind
Oscar Wilde

Methuen Drama Classical Greek Dramatists

Aeschylus Plays: One
(Persians, Seven Against Thebes, Suppliants,
Prometheus Bound)

Aeschylus Plays: Two
(Oresteia: Agamemnon, Libation-Bearers, Eumenides)

Aristophanes Plays: One
(Acharnians, Knights, Peace, Lysistrata)

Aristophanes Plays: Two
(Wasps, Clouds, Birds, Festival Time, Frogs)

Aristophanes & Menander: New Comedy
(Women in Power, Wealth, The Malcontent,
The Woman from Samos)

Euripides Plays: One
(Medea, The Phoenician Women, Bacchae)

Euripides Plays: Two
(Hecuba, The Women of Troy, Iphigeneia at Aulis,
Cyclops)

Euripides Plays: Three
(Alkestis, Helen, Ion)

Euripides Plays: Four
(Elektra, Orestes, Iphigeneia in Tauris)

Euripides Plays: Five
(Andromache, Herakles' Children, Herakles)

Euripides Plays: Six
(Hippolytos, Suppliants, Rhesos)

Sophocles Plays: One
(Oedipus the King, Oedipus at Colonus, Antigone)

Sophocles Plays: Two
(Ajax, Women of Trachis, Electra, Philoctetes)